BELLE TURNBULL

ON THE LIFE & WORK OF AN AMERICAN MASTER

Edited by David J. Rothman and Jeffrey R. Villines

ISBN: 978-0-9641454-9-8

Published by Pleiades Press & *Gulf Coast*

Department of English
University of Central Missouri
Warrensburg, Missouri 64093

Department of English
University of Houston
Houston, Texas 77204

Distributed by Small Press Distribution (SPD) and to subscribers
of *Pleiades: Literature in Context* and *Gulf Coast: A Journal of
Literature and Fine Arts.*

Series, series cover, and interior design by Martin Rock.
Volume design by Jeffrey R. Villines.

Cover photograph: Detail of "Belle Turnbull in her senior frock
    (1903)," courtesy of the Denver Public Library.

Unless otherwise noted, all photos are drawn from the same collection:
    The Belle Turnbull Papers, WH 414 (photo box), Western History, The
    Denver Public Library.

2 4 6 8 9 7 5 3 1

The Unsung Masters Series brings the work of great, out-of-print,
little-known writers to new readers. Each volume in the series
includes a large selection of the author's original writing, as well as
essays on the writer, interviews with people who knew the writer,
photographs, and ephemera. The curators of the Unsung Masters
Series are always interested in suggestions for future volumes.

Invaluable financial support for this project has been provided by the
National Endownment for the Arts, the Cynthia Woods Mitchell
Center for the Arts, and the Missouri Arts Council, a state agency.
Our immense gratitude to these organizations.

ART WORKS.

National
Endowment
for the Arts
arts.gov

Missouri
Arts Council
The State of the Arts

cynthia
woods
mitchellcenter
for the
arts
UNIVERSITY of HOUSTON

BELLE TURNBULL

ON THE LIFE & WORK OF AN AMERICAN MASTER

OTHER BOOKS IN THE UNSUNG MASTERS SERIES

2016
Beatrice Hastings: On the Life & Work of a Lost Modern Master
Edited by Benjamin Johnson and Erika Jo Brown

2015
Catherine Breese Davis: On the Life & Work of an American Master
Edited by Martha Collins, Kevin Prufer, & Martin Rock

2014
Francis Jammes: On the Life & Work of a Modern Master
Edited by Kathryn Nuernberger & Bruce Whiteman

2013
Russell Atkins: On the Life & Work of an American Master
Edited by Kevin Prufer & Michael Dumanis

2012
Nancy Hale: On the Life & Work of a Lost American Master
Edited by Dan Chaon, Norah Hardin Lind, & Phong Nguyen

2011
Tamura Ryuichi: On the Life & Work of a 20th Century Master
Edited by Takako Lento & Wayne Miller

2010
Dunstan Thompson: On the Life & Work of a Lost American Master
Edited by D.A. Powell & Kevin Prufer

2009
Laura Jensen: A Symposium
Edited by Wayne Miller & Kevin Prufer

THE UNSUNG MASTERS SERIES

CONTENTS

INTRODUCTIONS

"Too near heaven": Belle Turnbull, Poet of Colorado 15
DAVID J. ROTHMAN

Poet-Archive/Archive-Poet: Knowing Belle Turnbull through
Her Collections 29
JEFFREY R. VILLINES

A NOTE ON THE TEXT 38

FROM GOLDBOAT (1940)

[Opening/Dorn's Arrival] 42
[Dorn writes to Alicia] 44
[Dorn meets the Buffins] 46
Telegrams [I] 48
[Construction of the Goldboat] 49
[Leafy sees Alicia] 50
[Olsen] 53
Telegrams [V] 57
[The nightwatchman] 60
[The Goldboat settles] 62
Telegrams [VI] 65
[Dorn resigns/Conclusion] 67

FROM THE TENMILE RANGE (1957)

THE TENMILE RANGE

Foreword 70
Topography 71

Weather Conditions 72
Government 73
History 74

AT THAT POINT MR PROBUS

Time as a Well-Spring 75
Lunch Time in the Tunnel 76
Lyric Mood 77
Hardrock Miner 78
Mountain Woman 79
Address to a Tenderfoot 80
Miner's Pension 81
Opus 8 82
Summons to the Undertaker 83

FROM HOUSE IN THE VALLEY

Walls 84
Window on the Range 85
Dialog 86

FROM THE FOLK

In Those Rude Airs 87
Words About a Place 90

FROM TRAILS (1968)

High Trail 92
Observations Above Timberline 93
Short Lease 94
Long Lease 95
To Be Tacked on a Cabin Door 96
Pasque Flowers 97
Cycle: I. Sun Dance 98
Cycle: II. Easter Service 99
Bomber Over Breckenridge 100
These Who Shorn Return 101
By Stravinsky 102
Never the Words (A MONOLOG) 103

UNCOLLECTED & UNPUBLISHED POEMS

UNCOLLECTED PERIODICAL VERSE

Sonnet to Gertrude Buck 105
Song for Female Voices 106
Mountain-Mad 107
Reckoning 108

FROM THE LONG ARC

The Answer's in the Back 110
[Weather Report] 111
This Fir 112
Now the Slow Dawn 113
Epitaph for Clelia, a Spinster 114
The Long Arc 115
No Other Water 116
Small Stone 117
Inward Tussle for a Couple of Lines 118
Never the Words (A MONOLOG) [variant] 119

UNPUBLISHED MISCELLANY

Delinquent Tax List of Summit County 120
Answers to a Questionnaire 121
What is your religion? 122

"NOT TO BE PUBLISHED [DURING MY LIFETIME]"

Chant 123
Echo 124
Stone 125
Deep Music 126

PROSE

Autobiographical Note 128
from Gold Boats on The Swan: The Story of Ben Stanley Re-
vett, Gold Dredger 131

SCHOLARLY ESSAYS

Poverty Gulch and Mendicant Ridge: Prospecting for the
    Real Colorado 148
    GEORGE SIBLEY

A Way of Seeing: Belle Turnbull's Geography of Love.....162
    SUSAN SPEAR

Belle Turnbull: Poet under Quandary.....................172
    UCHE OGBUJI

Belle Turnbull's Western Narrative......................185
    DAVID MASON

NOTES AND ACKNOWLEDGMENTS

Notes on the Poetry....................................196
Works Cited Editorially................................200
About the Editors......................................201
Acknowledgements.......................................201

IMAGES

Belle Turnbull as a young girl 14

Belle Turnbull's handwriting 35

Layout in Belle Turnbull's *Goldboat* album, BTP ff. 6 37

"A functioning goldboat," The Helen Rich Papers, WH 348
    (photo box), Western History, The Denver Public Library. 41

The mountains over a snow-covered Breckenridge 69

Belle Turnbull by the stove (c. 1957) 91

"To Be Tacked on a Cabin Door" (with pinholes), BTP ff. 15 .. 96

Belle Turnbull with Helen Rich 104

The cabin at 9 French Street (c. 1959) 122

Belle Turnbull with Scotch terrier 127

Belle Turnbull in her senior frock (1903) 147

INTRODUCTIONS

One of the earliest surviving photographs of
Belle Turnbull.

"TOO NEAR HEAVEN": BELLE TURNBULL, POET OF COLORADO

Needs must harry the Tenmile now:
Hot in the channels behind the bone
The words are up and the drum beats over,
The drum beats over, the words must go.

Never along that range is ease:
Things are warped that are too near heaven,
Ink runs clotted down the pen,
Verse has the twist of timberline trees.
                    —Belle Turnbull, *"Foreword,"* The Tenmile Range

To say that Belle Turnbull, who lived from 1881 to 1970, is one of the strongest poets yet to emerge in Colorado might at first seem to condemn her to critical oblivion. While some American poets have leaped the regional fence to benefit from explicit, thematic self-identification with a place (Frost with New Hampshire, Jeffers with Carmel, Sandburg with Chicago, Whitman with New York, Berry with Kentucky, Dickinson with Amherst), for the lesser known the label "regionalist" presents a problem. Turnbull is indeed a poet who almost always wrote about a particular place at a particular time—the Colorado mountains in the age of mining, roughly 1875 to 1950. But she is one of those who might leap that regionalist fence if read right. For in writing of her specific place and time, she also made herself into a poet of the Emersonian sublime in its alpine dress. Her Tenmile Range, which runs past Breckenridge, Colorado, should figure as significantly in our collective imagination as Shelley's Mt. Blanc. She is a poet of Colorado, but also a substantial American poet, perhaps a great one.

In March of 2012, the historian Patricia Limerick, the Director of the Center of the American West at the University of Colorado at Boulder, invited me to give a lecture on the poetry of the American West to her undergraduate survey course. After this lecture, Janet Robertson, a friend of the Center, held a reception at her home, during which she asked me why I hadn't discussed Belle Turnbull in my remarks. I said I didn't talk about her because I had never heard of her. Robertson, an author herself of several books on Colorado mountaineering, passionately insisted I read Turnbull and guided me to some of her work, notably the Mr. Probus poems.

Like every editor, I see a tremendous amount of new work every year and approach it skeptically. And yet as soon as I read just a few pages of Turnbull I had the strange feeling that I was in the presence of a significant artist. Her work has an utterly modern music that is gritty and yet subtle, earthy yet refined, passionate yet cool. She is modern yet favors metrical verse. Her free verse always evinces a subtle ghost of meter and she knows how to tell a good story. Her best work is inextricably part of the Colorado mountains, yet always tied to larger concerns. I knew in part that it was significant because I could sense its beauty, yet the voice was so original I literally couldn't quite understand much of it at first.

Turnbull's originality is of tremendous significance to anyone who seeks to write about this part of the world, in poetry or in prose. Ambitious poetry and even clear thinking about any place in the present always requires a usable past, which is why Wallace Stegner wisely observed that "No place is a place until it has had a poet" (205). And when contemporary Colorado poets, by which I mean poets who want to write not only in Colorado but also of it in a visionary way, turn to the first couple of generations of English poetry in the state, the pickings can seem scant.

After Whitman, Longfellow, Katherine Lee Bates, Jeffers, and Thomas Hornsby Ferril, Colorado's early poetical identity in English drops off quickly. In fact, most of these poets were visitors and not residents: Whitman composed "Spirit that form'd this scene" in Platte Cañon, Colorado on a well-documented voyage through Missouri, Kansas, and Colorado in 1879. Longfellow never even saw the Mt. of the Holy Cross, but in 1879 wrote the posthumously published "The Cross of Snow," commemorating his late wife, based on descriptions and an etching. Katherine Lee Bates wrote "America the Beautiful" after ascending Pike's Peak in 1893 while on a sabbatical from Wellesley and teaching at Colorado College. Those purple mountain majesties above the fruited plane are description, not fancy. Robinson Jeffers wrote "Red Mountain" after one of his family's trips in the mid-1930s by car from Carmel to visit Mabel Dodge Luhan in Taos.

Of those I listed, only one poet was a resident of Colorado, and is perhaps the best-known poet of the state: Thomas Hornsby Ferril (1896-1988), a Yale Younger Poet (1926) who made his living in Denver as a journalist for many decades and was the state's fifth Poet Laureate, from 1979 to 1988. His sonnet "Here is a land where life is written in Water" has been imortalized in the Colorado state capital rotunda in a mural completed in 1940.

As for the rest, Levette J. Davidson, who edited the useful anthology *Poems of the Old West: A Rocky Mountain Anthology* is affectionate towards his poets, but writes that:

> Much of the poetry written in the Rocky Mountain West is deservedly forgotten. Too often it was composed by those who had nothing to say, who echoed the platitudes of popular Victorian versifiers, who used conventional topics and supposed poetic language. The books by such

> mistakenly ambitious souls are not much different from those by would-be but inadequate poets to be found in any other time and place. They are imitative and flat. (xii)

Of the more than 65 poets in Davidson's anthology, one of the few to stand out is Ferril, who is of a later generation than most of the others. Most of the rest is doggerel and newspaper verse, historically interesting but imaginatively weak. Turnbull is not included, which is a bit surprising, as she was fairly well-known at the time, having won a major national prize and published widely.

Among Davidson's anthologized poets, which include the well-known Eugene Field and some of the early, sentimentalist Colorado Poet Laureates,[1] one poet in particular will serve as an example of his critique: Alfred Castner King (1873-1941), the so-called blind poet of Colorado, who was perhaps the best-known poet of mining before Turnbull, and whose work she surely would have known. King was a miner blinded in an explosion near Ouray in 1900 who subsequently published two lengthy and popular books, *Mountain Idylls and other Poems* (1901) and *The Passing of the Storm and Other Poems* (1907). A typical example would be the first stanza of "The Ruined Cabin":

> There's a pathos in the solemn desolation
>   Of the mountain cabin singing in decay,
> With its threshhold overgrown with vegetation,
>   With its door unhinged and mouldering away.
> There's a weird and most disconsolate expression
>   In the sashless windows with their vacant stare,
> As in mute appeal, or taciturn confession
>   Of a wild and inconcolable despair.
>
> (Davidson 203-04)

It seems unfair to make King into Turnbull's whipping boy, but there it is. Turnbull begins to write her own poems of mining,

---

[1] The full list to date is Alice Polk Hill, 1919-1921; Nellie Burgett Miller, 1923-1952; Margaret Clyde Robertson, 1952-1954; Milford Shields, 1954-1975; Ferril; Mary Crow, 1996-2010; David Mason, 2010-2014; and now Joseph Hutchison, whose term ends in 2018.

miners, and mountains just a few decades later, but a single stanza on the same subject serves to show the shift from a merely regional poet to one whose consciousness opens upon a far greater imaginative universe:

> The tail of your eye, your nostrils know the ombre
> Of what was here. You know a stand of timber,
> Stout, having purple cones ambered with resin
> That roared along this chimney. And you know
> The smell of gold in a hole, perverse and somber.
>
> ("Words About a Place," TMR 53, UM 96)

The exuberant diction, the symbolist metaphors of collision ("the tail of your eye"), the puns ("ombre" for shadow but also close to "hombre" for the ghosts of the place), the rich half-rhymes, the knowing, instressed dislocations of meter, the rippling syntax all announce a very different poet. And yet, to give King his due, we can only measure the distance from him to her because we have his work, which is some of the best of its kind before her. No *King Lear* without *Gorboduc*.

Turnbull's haunting poem, the last in *The Tenmile Range*, continues for two more five-line stanzas. Suffice it to say, the poem rewards every rereading and only gives up its true subject slowly, almost successfully resisting. It approaches Stevens in its dense sweetness and sorrow. Set inextricably in the Colorado Rockies, it reaches far beyond them, to configure language, memory, history and art in a new place. Her sensibility has crossed a great divide from that of King and the hundreds of other versifiers who preceded her in writing about the same places and subjects. Where they are entertaining, she is crafty, thoughtful, extraordinarily sophisticated about language, a bit convoluted, allusive, precisely sensuous and, while not overtly literary, filled with allusive echoes.

Turnbull's life was relatively simple yet intriguing. She was born in 1881, in the middle of what may forever be the greatest cluster of American poetic births: seven years after Frost and Amy Lowell, three after Sandburg, two after Stevens, a year before Eliot, two before Williams, three before Teasdale, four before Pound, five before H.D., six before Jeffers and Marianne Moore. Her family moved from Clinton, New York, to Colorado Springs in 1890 because of her father's health. He became the Principal of the Colorado Springs High School and Turnbull presumably had a strong education there before attending Vassar. After graduating from college in 1904, she stayed in New York state for several years teaching school, then returned to Colorado Springs, where she eventually became chair of the English Department at the school where her father had been the Principal. She retired in 1937 and with Helen Rich, whom earlier biographical sketches have referred to as her "companion," moved to the mountain town of Frisco. Two years later the couple moved up to the nearby mining town of Breckenridge, situated at 9,600 feet at the foot of the Ten Mile Range, where they lived in a cabin at 9 French Street until Turnbull's death in 1970. Rich, who was several years younger, died just a few years later.

There may well be letters or other documents that indicate how Turnbull and Rich came to their decision to move up to the mountains in the 1930s. The archive of their papers at the Denver Public Library reveals astonishingly little of their earlier lives. It is fascinating to consider this cultivated and brainy lesbian couple living out their relatively uneventful and apparently happy lives in a high alpine mining town in decline, where they seemed to spend their untroubled days working various jobs, writing, and enjoying the mountains and their neighbors, who appear very carefully drawn in their works.

Of the two, Rich was the better-selling. Her first novel, *The Spring Begins*, was a best-seller in 1947, and she published another, *The Willow Bender*, in 1950, along with many short stories. Rich's novels, like Turnbull's poetry, show careful attention to the people and the place. Both clearly loved their town and the people in it, and worked hard to capture the rhythms of their speech, the nature of their work, and every other detail they could of how they lived their lives. Turnbull also published one novel, *The Other Side of the Hill*, with Crown in 1953. That work has interest, but only because of her poetry. It is hard to resist imagining Helen encouraging Belle to write prose, and Belle dutifully giving it her best effort, then turning to Helen and saying, "You know....I prefer verse."

In the end, Turnbull published just two books of poems and one chapbook during her life. While she had been writing ambitiously for some time while teaching, and had begun to publish fairly widely in journals, her writing only took off after her retirement, when she was already in her mid-50s. Her first book, *Goldboat*, is a 77-page novella in verse that appeared with Houghton Mifflin in 1940, when she was already almost 60. Her second was *The Tenmile Range*, a collection of lyrics written over many decades, which appeared with The Prairie Press, a small press in Iowa City edited by Caroll Coleman, in 1957, when she was 76. The final, rare publication, *Trails*, is a chapbook of just 15 poems. It appeared when she was 87, in 1968, from Gallimaufry Press in Bethesda, Maryland, in an edition of just a few hundred copies. *The Tenmile Range* was reprinted in 2007 by Marion Street Publishing company, a very small press that seems to have disappeared. The editor of the volume, Robert McCracken, did good spade work on Turnbull and also edited an e-book of her unpublished poems, which the Denver Public Librarians spoke of with a sniff, as, according to them, he copied and used unauthorized versions of her many poems from journals not yet collected. As this suggests, there is still quite a bit of work to do on her papers, slim as they may be.

Turnbull did enjoy fairly wide journal publication in the 1930s and later, along with some fame. She published fairly regularly in *Poetry* over several decades and in 1938 she won the journal's second annual Harriet Monroe Memorial Prize for a sequence that had appeared in the December 1937 issue, titled "At That Point Mr. Probus," which she later expanded and published as a section of *The Tenmile Range* (included in full here). She was in good company in *Poetry* that year; other prizewinners included H.D. and Dylan Thomas, for "Over Sir John's Hill."

As my co-editor Jeffrey R. Villines convincingly argues in his essay on Turnbull's archive, she was astonishingly careful about what she chose to preserve and how she did it, bringing to mind Dickinson's carefully organized fascicles. The collection of her papers in the Denver Public Library at first seems thin, until one realizes that almost every single page of it deserves publication. She carefully documented and organized her work, and completely understood what she was about. One entry from one of her scrapbooks (BTP ff. 26), carefully typed up and pasted in, reads:

> Reply to Ferril's frequent statement that after all mountains are only dirt, stone and such tangibles:
>
> Yes, but they are also symbols, unavoidably: his, mine, that lady poet's who ices them into wedding-cakes, that minister's who finds his God in one of them.
>
> And you, Tom, confess yourself when you say it is a matter for wonder that Helen Rich, that I, succeed in avoiding the use of them romantically. What you really mean is inherent in the term *fancy* as opposed to the term *imagination*; triteness vs originality.

An ambitious poet indeed, who knows her Coleridge and the crucial distinction he makes between faculties in the *Biographia Litteraria*. Whereas Ferril may have had trouble seeing beyond the fanciful treatment of the mountains in so much Colorado poetry before them, Turnbull very pointedly aimed to use what Coleridge called a "secondary imagination" of Colorado miners and their mountains to recreate them in art.[2]

---

[2] Coleridge discusses the primary and secondary imagination in contrast to fancy in Chapter XIII of the *Biographia Litteraria*:

> The Imagination then I consider either as primary, or secondary. The primary Imagination I hold to be the living power and prime agent of all

 (cont.)

To take just the "Mr. Probus" sequence, we find there a rich human and physical topography that had never appeared with such force before. Her Probus persona, a rather raunchy, tough, hardrock miner, may at first appear an odd alter ego for a diminutive lesbian and retired schoolteacher, but appearances can be deceiving. Turnbull presents him as an utterly believable character (as my co-editor points out, she forcefully insists on his verisimilitude), at the same time as she integrates facts about the lay of the land and the industry with tremendous sprezzatura, all the while unfurling verse in a tensile, instressed set of Petrarchan sonnets that feel both formally foregrounded yet colloquial.

Here is the first Mr. Probus poem, "Time as a Well-Spring," that finds Probus *in medias res*, contemplating his mortality:

> I thought, said Mr. Probus, there was time,
> Time by the dipperful, time lipping, flowing
> Out of some plenteous spring where I'd be going
> With my bright dipper, frosting it with rime,
> Hoarding no more than God would hoard a dime,
> Slipping time over my palate, careless blowing
> Drops off my mustache, wasting it full knowing
> There would be more, more always, soft and prime.
>
> I've lived some years at Stringtown, Probus said,
> Back in the mountain mining molybdenum,
> Gassed and sent in again and lined with lead.
> Seven years some few will last who stand the gaff.
> Sometimes where the machines bore, springs will come.
> I have to laugh, he said, I have to laugh.

(TMR 19, UM 78)

---

human perception, and as a repetition in the finite mind of the eternal act of creation in the infinite I AM. The secondary Imagination I consider as an echo of the former, co-existing with the conscious will, yet still as identical with the primary in the kind of its agency, and differing only in degree, and in the mode of its operation. It dissolves, diffuses, dissipates, in order to recreate: or where this process is rendered impossible, yet still at all events it struggles to idealize and to unify. It is essentially vital, even as all objects (as objects) are essentially fixed and dead.

FANCY, on the contrary, has no other counters to play with, but fixities and definites. The fancy is indeed no other than a mode of memory emancipated from the order of time and space; while it is blended with, and modified by that empirical phaenomenon of the will, which we express by the word Choice. But equally with the ordinary memory the Fancy must receive all its materials ready made from the law of association. (378)

This poem takes the same settings and situations of hundreds of previous mining poems, strikes them with a Symbolist wand, and creates something utterly new: the language feels both familiar and elevated at the same time. All the historical material is accurate. Stringtown was a real place near Leadville, not far from where molybdenum is still mined today. "To stand the gaff" refers to a comment made by a notorious mine boss, J. E. McClurg, during a strike by coal miners in Cape Breton, Nova Scotia, in 1925. When the miners continued their strike despite threats from management, McClurg apparently said "We hold all the cards ... they will have to come to us ... they can't stand the gaff," meaning that the hook of hunger and deprivation would eventually break them. The phrase was so well-known in mining circles that a number of songs were written that tell the story and incorporate the phrase to indicate the miners' resistance to such tactics. To say that a miner is "gassed" seems clear enough, although the locution seems anachronistic now and appears to have been used more frequently in the United Kingdom than here.

Again and again, whether the subject is mining, weather, geology, botany, topography, and more, Turnbull pulls off the same virtuosic turn, combining precise observations with lyrical language and crisp, compressed verse. Her free verse novel *Goldboat* tells a story of greed and love in the mountains, but revolves around the business of gold dredging, and shows tremendous research into the industry and its financial transactions, including the shady ones. She also looks directly at the danger and violence that could accompany mining. There is enough action and story in *Goldboat* for a strong screen treatment.

Despite having good publications and even reviews, Turnbull was no self-promoter and the books did not sell well. Turnbull knew herself and recognized that she not only lived out of the way but wrote in an unfashionable mode. In a letter to her publisher, Carroll Coleman, in early 1962, she wrote, accurately echoing Hopkins as she characterizes her own work, that her poetry is "not in any style now in favor among either poets or publishers. You see, I'm still a pushover for compactness and inbuilt rhythms" (BTP ff. 10).

Yet Turnbull did find highly significant readers, among them May Sarton, James Merrill and David Jackson, and William Meredith, along with Ferril, who was a close friend. In her careful way, she kept correspondence from many of them, and Meredith's 1957 review of *The Tenmile Range* in *The New York Times* is the most prescient criticism ever written of her work. Discussing "Time as a Well-Spring," Meredith argues that "We feel the experience in this poem because we are not allowed to generalize it away. The man, his speech and the source of his imagery are highly particular. The 'message' of the poem can only be apprehended dramatically, because that is the only way it is stated [...] it suggests the general excellence of 'The Ten Mile Range.'"

It takes time to learn how to read Turnbull, as it should with any original poet. She is rich, she frequently aims for the sublime, and she is original. Consider the poem that serves as an epigraph for this essay, "Foreword," which is the first lyric in *The Tenmile Range*. At first, and for quite some time, I was unclear just what the "needs" were that might "harry the Tenmile now." And then the obvious struck me: they are forthrightly Turnbull's own needs, her tangled, complex, loving, ecstatic urge to capture such magnificence in words, until "Ink runs clotted down the pen, / Verse has the twist of timberline trees." And it is in exactly this way, with the passionate integrity of a secondary imagination, that she always moves towards capturing the mountains, the fauna that cloak them, and the people who try to live in them. Even in an acknowledgment of expressive failure she moves towards what she loves, seeking never to resolve such anxiety, but to achieve it.

This brief introduction, the work excerpted in this volume, and the critical essays on Turnbull by Jeffrey R. Villines, George

Sibley, Susan Spear, Uche Ogbuji and David Mason, only begin to scratch the surface. Readers should view them as attempts to start a conversation. Villines and I agree that Turnbull's careful self-curating of what she left us means that, thin as it is, almost all of it deserves to see print. Her uncollected verse, her unpublished work, and her notebooks reward the reader on every page. Nothing is merely informational. She even typed and organized a section of her manuscripts titled "Fragments." And they're good: "And dropped my burdens like a sunlit tree / After long snow" (BTP ff. 22).

Another section deserves special note. One manuscript bears the section title page "Not for publication [during my lifetime]." The words "during my lifetime" have been heavily scored out, though are still legible. There is no explanation, and yet the poems are preserved. Jeffrey and I thought and thought about this, and finally agreed that Turnbull would not have left us these poems if she did not in fact mean for them to be published. Many are quite beautiful and mysterious. If they contained something personal that Turnbull wanted not to express, that is unclear, although some, such as "Echo," might be interpeted as love poems for Helen:

> Once
> Across the black marsh-country
> Measureless between death and burial
> Swung your unconquered voice
> Tolling my name.
>
> (BTP ff. 22, UM 124)

Yet, whose voice is this? It is, after all, an echo, so is it the poet merely speaking to herself? Why choose not to publish it, and then carefully preserve it in a highly organized manuscript? In any event, these lovely poems and many hundreds of pages of other unpublished and worthy material await more work. All of Turnbull's published, uncollected and unpublished poetry and nonfiction prose would fit into one substantial volume, but that goes far beyond what we can accomplish here. There is a great deal of archival, biographical, historical and scholarly work to do. All we can offer here is a beginning.

When it comes to the contest between authenticity and imagination in poetry, the imagination always wins. All that matters is that a poem is strong enough to be convincing. Shakespeare's unnamed island of exile in *The Tempest* seems far more real than any number of real landscapes which are forgettable even though they may be sincerely described, and his fair Verona, which he never visited and where Italians speak English, is so convincing a setting that other strong writers have themselves been able to translate it into everything from the South Pacific to Brooklyn and back to England itself.

To view the poetry of place as poetry first and place second, which is to let the strongest poets guide us into the place as an imaginative trope, rather than a discursive reflection of the authentic, is to cut a Gordian knot, and thereby return us to the poems as poems. When we keep this imaginative power foremost in mind and then ask again what the strongest poetry of Colorado might include, the answer becomes simple: the strongest poems about the place and the spirits of the place. Belle Turnbull is in the very first rank of those poets to date, and the Colorado that she gives us not only sparkles with authentic historical and factual reality, but convinces emotionally and even spiritually, building a bridge from an American landscape to the American sublime. She is indeed an unsung master, an American poet who deserves and will reward our attention, an artist who belongs in the first rank of those who have realized the American sublime so close to heaven it clots ink, here in Colorado.

David J. Rothman

WORKS CITED

Coleridge, Samuel Taylor. *Biographia Litteraria, or, Biographical Sketches of my Literary Life and Opinions, from the Second London Edition.* Edited by Henry Nelson Coleridge, William Gowans, 1852.

Davidson, Levette J., editor. *Poems of the Old West: A Rocky Mountain Anthology.* Denver UP, 1951. Kessinger Publishing reprint.

Meredith, William. "Renewal of Experience Is the Key." *New York Times Book Review*, 26 May 1957: p. 4.

Stegner, Wallace. *Where the Bluebird Sings to the Lemonade Springs: Living and Writing in the West.* Random House, 1992.

POET-ARCHIVE/ARCHIVE-POET: KNOWING BELLE TURNBULL THROUGH HER COLLECTIONS

"It's a revealing thing, an author's index of his own work."
Kurt Vonnegut, Cat's Cradle

The December, 1937, issue of *Poetry* not only included Belle Turnbull's award-winning Mr. Probus poems,[1] but also this brief biographical gloss:

> BELLE TURNBULL was born in Hamilton, New York, but since the age of seven has lived in Colorado Springs. She warns us not to object to the present group of sonnets "on the ground that miners couldn't talk that way. Some of them do." She also informs us that "Mr. Probus works in the Climax Molybdenum mines, and Stringtown is a part of Leadville." ("Notes" 173)

Unremarkable as this paragraph may seem, it is nonetheless an exemplary introduction to Turnbull. The actual biographical data is scant, doing little more than positioning her in Colorado. Yet while Colorado would prove a significant theme in Turnbull's poetry, this gloss reveals more oblique themes and artistic values which Turnbull would explore through the remainder of her long career. It also sets the tone for the efficient organization she imposed on her own legacy, as evident in the slim but rich archives of her work in the Denver Public Library.

---

[1] This sonnet cycle was expanded in TMR and has been reproduced in its entirety in this volume: UM 75-83.

UNPACKING THE GLOSS

Consider Turnbull's assertion about the speech habits of Colorado miners. This is reminiscent of Twain's discussion of the dialects he uses in *Huckleberry Finn*, in which he indicates the variety of accents he has carefully reproduced, lest the reader mistakenly believe "that all these characters were trying to talk alike and not succeeding" (7). For Twain, such a criticism would reveal no failing as a writer on his part—rather, it would reveal a failing in the critic to perceive the American South as something more than a laughable monoculture. Similarly, in Turnbull's assertion that "some miners do" speak the way that she has them speak in the Probus poems, she is not just defending her craft or her attention to detail against charges of artifice, she is also defending her Breckenridge neighbors against charges of shallowness and dullness. From this we can see that Turnbull does not merely inhabit Breckenridge, but participates in and identifies with it as a community.

However, in defending her diction, Turnbull makes the corollary assertion that there is something distinctly lyrical *to* her poetry. After all, why should a hypothetical reader object to the presented reality of the miners' speech if there isn't that trace of the extraordinary—the poetic—to raise that prospective reader's suspicions? This is not only a reminder that Belle Turnbull is a poet, it also reflects a persistent quirk apparent in her prose: an apophatic tendency to elevate her accomplishments while auspiciously downplaying them. We can see this at work in Turnbull's "Autobiographical Note" (BTP ff. 5; UM 128-130) in which her repeated acknowledgment of what her Vassar education failed to prepare her for nonetheless underscores that education (UM 129). Similarly, in a February, 1962, letter to publisher Carroll Coleman, she "apologizes" for the gaucheness of her poems: "most of the items are not in any style now in favor among either poets or publishers. You see, I'm still a pushover for compactness and inbuilt rhythms" (BTP ff. 10). Even as she seems to acknowledge her style as outmoded, she instantly positions this as a result of superior craft—an aesthetic more enduring than what may currently be "in favor." Her ambitious modesty evokes the freelancer's dual needs to trumpet her work in order to sell it even while she maintains the humility needed to revise and edit.

Finally, we have the sentences which state the setting of the poems. Here we see a poet who is also a diligent researcher: Probus is not some cipher of a character working in a generic mine in a featureless community—he enjoys a detailed existence in a particular place, where he participates in a precise form of mining common to a specific Colorado locale.[2] Though Probus himself is an invention, Turnbull attests that the invented qualities are slight. Probus is so plausible a figure, he may just as well be real.

It seems clear that Turnbull makes these claims to forestall an anticipated reaction from readers. However, there is also an insistence on receiving credit and recognition for the research she has done. Brief as this gloss is, she is unwilling to let her research lie invisible behind her poetry. Perhaps this is because she thought of her research as not just something to facilitate expression, but rather as an additional means of expression. In her research, there is a care for facts and careful organization which can help us better understand her achievement as a poet, and this is readily apparent in her slim but well-organized archive.

THE BELLE TURNBULL PAPERS

The Belle Turnbull Papers are housed in the Western Heritage Collection at the Denver Public Library in Denver, Colorado. The collection is on the small side—a single document box and a single photo box. However, unlike many of the archives I have worked with, there is no single document which causes me to wonder, "Who would ever use *that*?"[3]

---

[2] Even the choice of mineral is telling. Whereas gold- or coal-mining may have been more recognizable or iconic, it would also have been more generic. There is something very specific to Probus's occupation, and that specificity ties the poems even more firmly to the realities of Colorado.

[3] As a counter-example, the Secretary of State Series in the James Madison Papers contains numerous bank draughts used to pay minor functionaries. These draughts are all of a kind, and many are identical in all except for their dates. None of these documents is worthless, but their documentary value tends to be as parts of a trend. As individual documents, their significance is greatly reduced outside of how they either further or disrupt those trends.

No document in the Belle Turnbull Papers is superfluous; each seems to have been saved for a reason. The collection does not hide its secrets with clutter and ephemera.

However, this can be a hindrance as well as a blessing, for there are many facets of Turnbull's daily life and creative process which we will never know without such ephemera. Household bills, no matter how dreary to read, could have been arranged to tell us much about life in the Breckenridge cabin she shared with Helen Rich. Rejection letters from poetry journals could have constructed a narrative about how she became aware of and approached her markets. Her correspondence folder is thin, as Turnbull kept copies of very few of her outgoing letters, and consequently we have an imcomplete picture of the conversations she had with poets all over America. This is to say nothing of the volumes on Turnbull's aesthetic priorities that could have been gleaned from a greater surviving sampling of her hand-emended manuscript pages. And with Belle Turnbull, we have almost none of that material.[4]

But no archive can be perfect, no matter how skilled, diligent, or discriminating the archivist. This is largely because the true medium of the archivist isn't documentation, but space; there is never sufficient space in any archive to preserve all that deserves preservation, and so an archivist's job is one of artistic triage. However, if the paper-trail of Belle Turnbull had to be miniaturized, then it could have fared no better than it has done at the Denver Public Library.

The collection changed hands several times before it became the entity now in Denver. We know from its provenance statement that it was processed in 2007. The documents were originally donated to the library by Alex Warner in 1971, shortly after the death of Helen Rich, who had herself come into possession of them upon Turnbull's death in 1970. At any or all stages in

---

[4] We do have a slight but engaging glimpse into this in the poem "Never the Words (A MONOLOG)" (T 15; UM 103). Not only is this poem about her aesthetic process, but when placed alongside its variants "Inward Tussel for a Couple of Lines" (BTP ff. 12; UM 118) and "Never the Words (A MONOLOG) [variant]" (BTP ff. 12; UM 119), a meta-commentary forms as we see that even her reflections on her aesthetic process are subject *to* that process.

between, the collection could well have shrunk and changed. And while proving the individual influence of these various hands could be the work of a lifetime, the most intriguing archival decisions were likely made by Turnbull herself.

TURNBULL AS RESEARCHER AND ARCHIVIST

Whether it is the material details of gold-dredging practices, the qualities of local flora and fauna, or observations on area "tax delinquents" (derelict gold dredges), the effect of Turnbull's research on her poetry is quickly apparent.[5] And while any conscientious writer can be expected to educate herself on her subject matter, especially when she seems so invested in recreating her region in her writing, Belle Turnbull's scholarly diligence approaches academic rigor. In her thorough prose biography of Ben Stanley Revett (excerpted UM 131-146)—a noted mine owner who had operated in her area—we see a Turnbull whose research has gone beyond the needs of her poetry. Her research on Revett had been part of her preparation for writing her 1940 book-length narrative poem *Goldboat,* and while we can see its general effect on that poem in the descriptions of dredging practices or even specific incidents that had occurred at dredging operations, the Revett biography reveals that she used but a fraction of the information gathered. On the one hand, this reduction is a testament to Turnbull's understanding of poetry as an art form of what isn't said. On the other, her decision to spin her excess information into an article for a Colorado historical magazine suggests an enthusiasm for the subject matter beyond how it served her narrative, and a pride in the act of discovery itself.

In her papers, there survive numerous artifacts from her various fact-finding missions. In one folder is a pair of neatly

[5]Though perhaps not even as visible as it could have been. In a 1940 letter exchange with attorney Carl Kaiser, we see him advising her on the legality of publishing poetry which quotes from archived letters and documents. This exchange not only speaks to Turnbull's awareness of the practical limitations of archival poetry, but also suggests that her source documents may have been intended to hold a more prominent place in her work.

written tables chronicling the monthly rain- and snowfall in Breckenridge over the course of seventeen years (BTP ff. 33). The differing qualities of ink in various parts of these tables suggests they were compiled over the course of numerous research trips. As to what their purpose was, what project they were supposed to inform, we cannot confidently say—but their management is meticulous. Here, or in the annotations for the Revett biography in which she communicates her manuscript and periodical sources for that article (and, presumably, for *Goldboat* as well), or in the poem "Delinquent Tax List of Summit County" (BTP ff. 20; UM 120), we have a slight indication of the hours spent poring through old periodicals, or straining her eyes over handwritten letters and journals, or navigating a labyrinth of public records.

It is likely Turnbull's experience with the archives and papers of others played directly into certain decisions she made about the management of her own. It is impossible to say with confidence just how many of the features of the Turnbull Papers come directly from her, and how many have been added (or deleted) over the course of a slow document-based game of telephone, but there are certain things which must have originated with her.

For one thing, the vast majority of her documents are typed. When I lamented a dearth of manuscript pages earlier, this was not an indication of the absence of poems or letters. These things are there, but they are almost always typed (often in duplicate). As a result, Turnbull's pages are eminently readable. Often, the unpublished poems in her papers are preserved in duplicate— with a white "clean" copy and a less clear yellow copy. The yellow copies often have minor alterations in Turnbull's unmistakeable hand, but there must have been other pages, handwritten pages— more heavily emended drafts of which the typed poems are the transcriptions or final products—but for the most part we do not have them. We do have a couple of notebooks which give us a peek at her process, but even many entries in these notebooks are typed. One in particular is a book of fragments, lines and couplets which she was growing into longer poems. The fragments aren't simple handwritten notations, but have been typed, then neatly pasted or taped in place. As for the lone surviving notebook that has been filled with handwritten notes, Turnbull provides it with a neat hand-written index. All of her notebooks are meticulously organized, and her handwriting is both neat and regular, if a little small at times.

A sample of Belle Turnbull's handwriting in a copy of *The Tenmile Range* gifted to the National Jewish Hospital (now National Jewish Health) in Denver.

There are numerous notebooks and commonplace books in the papers, and no two are alike in style or construction. Some are elegant albums, bought expressly for archival projects and some had been repurposed from out-of-date calendars she had been given by her insurance agent, but none of them are haphazardly arranged. Most of them revolve around a specific theme: fragments, a commonplace book of quotes and poems (also typed and pasted), an anthology she was working on, and so on. Here we see an organizing impulse, a desire for everything to be sorted and orderly. Was she so meticulous in her organization simply because that was her personality, or was this neatness in reaction to some haphazard collections she had had to contend with in her previous research—driving her to spare some future biographer or anthologist the frustration of decoding an unsteady hand?

The arrangement of one interesting volume suggests organization, not just from personal fastidiousness, but with an eye toward eventual publication. This is the album devoted to the publication of *Goldboat* (BTP ff. 3). It begins with the 1938 letter in which R. N. Linscott of Houghton Mifflin reached out to her to ask if she had considered publishing a book. From there, she pursued a conversation with her future publishers in which they persuaded her not to publish *The Tenmile Range* (then titled *The Ten Mile District*) just yet, arguing a collection would sell better after a novel. We have fragments of her research, her publication contract, her galleys, and numerous other documents leading to the volume's publication. After that, there are advertisements for the book as well as reviews. These reviews are especially interesting because they are not all glowing, but have nonetheless been carefully preserved. One in particular, written by Sarah Henderson Hay for *The Saturday Review*, describes the plot as "trite" and "difficult to follow." "It is the reviewer's opinion that the medium of poetry detracts rather than adds to the force of the work," she states. This is a firm verdict to pass on any narrative poet, but particularly for a first book. Had this album been compiled entirely as a salve to Belle Turnbull's vanity, this review would be an odd inclusion. However, its presence suggests an archivist's valuation of preserving an accurate picture over inventing a favorable one. As a result, the album is more than a book of pleasing remembrances—it is also a precise documentary history of the publication process and the early reception of her breakout work.

Another telling feature of the papers—put in place by Turnbull herself and suggesting an informed awareness of the needs of some future, hypothetical researcher—is found among her photographs. Photographs can be a mixed bag in terms of their usefulness as sources: on the one hand, they are so densely packed with information—for instance, the postures of figures speak to the relationship *of* those figures, and clothing can tell us about class, wealth, or values—that their examination makes possible a dozen insights that would have been entirely

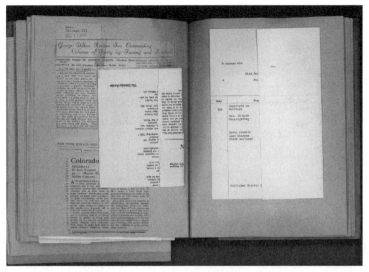

A single layout from the *Goldboat* album. Like Thomas Jefferson's own copy of his *Notes on the State of Virginia*, many entries are folded and layered, resisting a perfect photographic reproduction.

inaccessible without them. On the other hand, if the subject of the photograph cannot be linked (even indirectly) to the subject of research, the evidentiary value approaches nil.

It appears Turnbull was aware of this paradox, and acted on it. Among her photographs is an album of very old photos, only slightly newer than daguerreotypes, of well-dressed relatives posing primly for picture day. We know the subjects of these photos by name and by their relationship to Belle Turnbull, not because David and I performed some exhaustive detective work, but because, at some point, Turnbull carefully indexed this album.

She did not tape or glue labels to the pages, or otherwise mar them. She wrote out, in the neat, tight hand of her adulthood, a carefully numbered list of the subject of every photograph in the album, then neatly folded this sheet between the album's pages. This precise yet non-invasive means deftly preserves not only the associations of the materials, but the materials themselves.

Does this prove that Belle Turnbull was thinking of her posthumous readers? Not conclusively. But it speaks to her ambition as a poet. She was not one who wrote solely for her own idle amusement. A paragon of poetic professionalism, she always had an eye on her name and reputation. Even late in life, she persisted in searching for a market for her unpublished volume, *The Long Arc.* Belle Turnbull never quit, but instead martialed her every resource and talent towards the management of her career—a career which extends even to this day, in the form of her unusually well-organized legacy.

A NOTE ON THE TEXT

The volume you are now reading is only an introduction, and a slim one at that. As such, there were countless times when some potential project casually revealed itself to David or me as we worked through Turnbull's archive, but could not be made to fit within the needs or scale of this book. We both considered using the Unsung Masters Series as a venue to bring all of her poetry back into print, including her two books and one chapbook, her uncollected magazine verse, and *The Long Arc*—her final, unpublished collection. To do this, though, would have been to steal from the other sections, and consequently give our readers too narrow a picture. Other projects we spoke about or otherwise considered were studies of Turnbull's prose, her journals, her correspondence, including her substantial interest in other gay poets (whom she seems to have sought out) and what that suggests about her own work, or an attempt to uncover the rationale behind the anthology of poetry she had been putting together. Any of these projects would have been interesting and useful, but would also have pulled this volume in too specific a direction, undercutting the generality on which its introductory aim depends. But nothing is lost; these and other potential lines of inquiry, all carefully preserved for us by Turnbull, await the interested scholar who would make her way to Denver and peruse the archives as we have done. And this is to say nothing of the numerous critical endeavors waiting in the poetry itself, independent of any further archival study: eco-critical readings of

Turnbull's Colorado, aesthetic articulations of the various poetic traditions she partakes in or subverts, questions of narrative, questions of lyricism, or questions of form—along with countless other interesting critical and theoretical modes of inquiry. There are entire careers to be made in Belle Turnbull.

Owing to the aforementioned dearth of manuscript pages, our choices for copy-texts were limited. We have necessarily deferred to previously published forms of the included poems. For those previously unpublished poems, taken directly from her papers, we have generally followed the clear "white copy" of each poem, unless the "yellow copy" bears some meaningful alteration in Turnbull's hand. These alterations are rare enough that they are usually commented on in the Notes section of this book.

We have arranged this volume simply: The first three sections each correspond with one of the poetical volumes Turnbull published in her lifetime (*Goldboat*, *The Tenmile Range*, and *Trails*). The fourth section is for uncollected or unpublished poems; the fifth is for her prose, correspondence, and reviews. In the sixth section, you will find four new scholarly essays.

Belle Turnbull: On the Life & Work of an American Master uses two systems of annotations: one for poetry and one for prose. Explanatory notes for the poetry have all been placed in a single, discreet section, consistent with current practices of verse publication; the poems will not be marred by any on-page apparatus indicating the presence of such a note in this final section. Readers struck by an odd instance of mining terminology, Colorado flora, or general antiquarian flourishes will do well to check this section in the event their needs have been anticipated. This is also the section where readers can find citations for works referenced in the editorial annotations.

For the prose, we have employed footnotes and parentheticals. Footnotes address editorial explanations or authorial asides. Sources are acknowledged with parentheticals, which refer to a Works Cited list on the last page of each essay. The style guide for these citations (both in-text and bibliographic) is the *MLA Handbook* (8th ed.), with the exception of those sources which come directly from the Belle Turnbull Papers, which are cited using the preferred citation of the Denver Public Library, in accordance to their terms of use.

Furthermore, this colume uses persistent sigla to avoid needless repetition in the citation of Turnbull's books:

GB   *Goldboat.* Houghton Mifflin, 1940.

TMR   *The Tenmile Range.* Prairie Press, 1957.

FSH   *The Far Side of the Hill.* Crown Publishers, 1953.

T   *Trails.* Gallimaufry Press, 1968.

BTP   The Belle Turnbull Papers, WH 414 (document box), Western History, The Denver Public Library.[6]

In addition to the above references to Turnbull's books, the siglum UM refers to poems and other materials which appear in the present Unsung Masters volume.

Jeffrey R. Villines

WORKS CITED

Hay, Sara Henderson. "The New Poetry." *The Saturday Review,* 15 Feb. 1941: pp. 7, 12.

"Notes on Contributors." *Poetry,* vol. 51, no. 3, Dec. 1937: p. 173.

Twain, Mark. *The Adventures of Huckleberry Finn (Tom Sawyer's Comrade).* Charles L. Webster and Company, 1885.

---

[6] Often, a file folder number ("ff.") will be used alongside this siglum to indicate the specific location of a document.

A period gold dredge. Note both the complex pump mech-
anism and the precarious positioning of the crewman on the
mast.

[Opening/Dorn's Arrival]

Over the Great Divide unrolls the highway
And cars go wagging their tails among the thunders,
Range to range stitching, weather to weather.
In half a day you can hem up the watershed
And rush on the prairie or race on the desert again
Unaware of the infinite clues of legend,
The featherstitching of roads that thread the meadows,
Follow the gulches, follow the mountain pattern.

Or a man may twist his wheel where a wild road feathers
Under a range that marches on a valley,
Turn and be gone away to Rockinghorse country,
Wind through the park beside its swaggering river,
Creep on a shelf around a rocky shoulder,
Check in a pasture, by a waterpit
Under a rocksnake of cold blue cobbles mounded.

Still pond, no moving. And a wooden bird,
A squad, hightailing monstrous waterwidgeon
Diving its chain of spoonbills down and under
Red-rusted in a turquoise pit.
No moving. And no sound from the grotesque
Impossible of vision.
                        Only the wind,
The long, the diamond wind disturbs that water.

There wasn't any widgeon or rocksnake
When young John Dorn came seething into the district
Easing the tires of his palpitant new roadster
Along the corduroy through the Goose Pasture,

With his negro cook adrift and undone in the tonneau
And a goldscale riding hard on her jellied bosom.

Over the valley grassed and bare of timber,
Sparsely graced by June bouquets of aspen,
Over the buckbush hovering hidden channels,
Over the soil's core washed from the side gulches,
Over the pits and scars of the first deflowering,
The old quick rape of grassroots, traveled Dorn's eyes
In this first ride, to probe for gold at bedrock.

Leafy Buffin saw him drive under the cabin
That arches an eyebrow on the river bench.
She told her pop when he swung down out of timber,
The minute he straddled squaretoed over the doorsill.
Said there sat God himself in a buzzwagon.
Said he was color of rusty gold, sat easy,
Sailed right up the grade and into Rockinghouse
Like the earth was his and the waters under the earth.
Shook her smoky hair and twinkled her eyelids,
Said he could have it for her, and the fence and the fenceposts.

"Mind your maidenhood," Ike Buffin said to her,
And combed his ginger hair with square-ended fingers,
"That ain't no common folks, he's company boss
For that new outfit that's hogged up all the placers,
Ditmar's outfit that ripped out the guts of the Huntress,
Half of Africa, left em holdin the bag.
Old Squeezem Ditmar's the horns and the hoofs of that outfit.
Goin to whack out a boat that'll gore our gulches,
A stinkin, clankin son of a bee of a goldboat.
Like president, like boss, so now I tell you."

[Dorn writes to Alicia]

Dorn enters Rockinghorse with a flourish, "galloping in" to the area of his new management, where a cabin is already being constructed for the workers. An enthused Dorn sits down to write a letter to Alicia Ditmar, who is both his sweetheart and the daughter of Samuel Ditmar, president of the Summit Gold Company, the outfit which employs Dorn.

"Alicia sweeting:
                Enter now Adventure.
The teeth of the Rockinghose range grin through the window
On your engineer, that we fledged in the soft coast country,
That rose from his tub to mince about on field work.
They grin when he dabs his face in a teacup of icewater,
When he sleeps in cotton blankets over a mattress
That only a horse could find in his heart to cherish.
Before long, my girl those teeth shall have something to bite on,
The day your fine young lad that used to say *Right sir,*
And I will see your design is carried out sir,
Struts on his dredge and gives the command to dig.

"Girl, ever since you gave me the bud of your promise
I have pranced on my hind legs…"

                           The pen stopped running.
Dorn's eyes roached back in the rust-red roughened hair,
His eyes dreamed on the snow-silvered screen
Beyond the window.
              His own girl Alicia
Was she his own though   There was a flitting poise
About her body   like a hummingbird
Never in hand a moment. How should a man
Ever dare to take those delicate bones
Wholly into his arms   or dare to crush
The dainty flesh of her mouth

                              a mouth dissolving
Fading oddly on the silver screen
Into her father's mouth. You never remembered
Samuel Ditmar's face except his mouth
That was etched with lines of acid into metal.
Mouth that opened once on a word of grace:
"And since my daughter risks experiment,
And since your father died in Africa
To prove a dredge of mine, I play your ardor
Against the Rockinghourse…"
                              Dorn shook his pen,
Blankly eyed his fresh blot on the dingy pattern,
Wrote again:
                    "Girl, there was once a book
Written in runes of fire and ice and rock,
Scattered by floods and buried deep in the gulches.
Today I have begun to piece its fragments
Timberline to valley, and I vow to you
A golden locket for the earliest fruit
Of consummation…"

[Dorn meets the Buffins]

*In the days after he arrives, Dorn comes to know the region
and is convinced that the gold is plentiful. His first task is to
see to the construction of a goldboat, the mechanism used to
dredge waterways for gold. It is in the process of this that he
meets sawmill operator Ike Buffin, whose daughter, Leafy, had
noticed Dorn immediately upon his arrival. Dorn joins the
Buffins, just after Ike has shared with his daughter his less-
than-flattering impressions of the new manager.*

                      "I seen them,"
Said Buffin. "They aim to sink a pipe and drill
In the Goose Pasture, where you could spit from my sawmill.
I see young Dorn in his leather leggins adancin
Like some red Indian brave preparin his warbags.
And here was this ganglin bird, I couldn't place him,
Messin round and gearin up his machinery.
I'm sure God settin nice for a piece of business,
Maybe I'll do some good with this cussed sawmill."

He bent to splutter into the washbasin.
Then through the doorway was heard a bumblehumming,
And there stood Dorn, poised on the balls of his feet
easy and cool as a king, and the light wind ruffling
The rusty gold of his head, that was bared to greet them.
His eyes gold-brown looked out at them frank and friendly
To melt the icicle of mountain pride.

"My name's John Dorn," he said. "Heard you say sawmill."
He looked toward Leafy, saw her stand to meet him
Like the sweep of a young fir. "Well, lumber's my errand.
I want to build the scow for my dredge and the housing
Out of your native wood."

                   "Hi, go easy," said Buffin.
"Eat your supper with us, and then we'll talk lumber."

"So do," said Leafy low, and her eyelids quiet.
"So do."

       They sat long into the evening,
And Thedus growled in the lodge at her dinner spoiling.
And a boat rose plank by plank and rode the waters,
And Leafy wove her darning under the oil lamp.

Night after night the gravel crunched on the trail.
Night after night Dorn's hot young brain went scything
Problem to problem over the crackling blueprints,
And Buffin's shrewder native wit winnow
Behind, and Leafy smile at her mending.

Out of their minds wild feathered seeds went spinning.
What does he want, thought Buffin under the oil lamp,
And her with no more fear than a rose blowing
Shows to the bees   I never seen a boy
Pay her so little mind   Postmaster figures
He's courtin a girl back East   He's no damn tomcat
If I'm to judge

          What does she want, thought Dorn,
What does she smile about above her needle
Her mouth is wide   too wide   Her eyes are smoky
She is as quiet as a balsam spreading
She is not pretty   She is woman   is woman.

What does he want, thought Leafy at her mending,
With bilgestrakes and with keelsons and with bowlogs
A god that can hum like some great big golden bullfrog

Telegrams [I]
This portion immediately follows the previous.

DORN, MANAGER
TO DITMAR, PRESIDENT

Lumber under contract
Scow and housing ditto

DORN TO DITMAR

First drillhole down
Extraordinary values
Flattened nugget
Thirty-five ounces

JOHN TO ALICIA

Out of first nugget
Comes your golden locket

DITMAR TO DORN

Send me first nugget   stop
And every nugget after   stop
Bait allimportant

[Construction of the Goldboat]

Preliminary drilling reports are promising, but subsequent reports return lesser yields. Nonetheless, Dorn is convinced of the profitability of the operation, and sends optimistic reports to the Company. Regardless, Samuel Ditmar pledges to send Dorn less than he has requested to build the goldboat, and Dorn becomes aware of his boss's reputation for stinginess.

                    Now from that point at center
Shot out the giant radii of labor.
Sixty-two feet long the stout spud timbers
Grown from the core of ages out in Oregon
Hillside to skidway, skidway down to sawmill,
Sawmill to widegauge, widegauge down to narrow,
Came edging round the hairpins over Arctic,
Came bumping down behind the swink of oxen
To hold the dredge at anchor.

                    Out of Ohio
Out of the minehead, out of smelter, foundry,
Clattered iron organs over the prairie,
Over the mountains toward the swarming meadow
Where nerve and skill and sweating force were mingling
To build a goldboat.

[Leafy sees Alicia]

Throughout construction, Leafy has lingered near the work site hoping to catch sight of Dorn, but he is too occupied in his management duties and correspondence with Ditmar, who has informed Dorn that he is coming in for an inspection of the new boat, and will be bringing Alicia along. The boat begins operation, and produces its first gold leaf, which John Dorn takes as a good sign of things to come. However Thedus, his black cook, is less assured. Meanwhile, in preparation for the Ditmars' visit, Thedus hires on extra staff—Leafy Buffin.

That day when Leafy came to serve the lodge
The kitchen glowed against an icebright morning;
Edge of autmun is sharp under the spearheads.

Thedus poked at her stove, and her sidelong eyes
Measured and measured again the girl beside her,
The dark hair smoky-curled, the clear face
Above the blue-starred print, the uncowed balance,
Saw that she was good.

                    "I see," said Leafy,
"Their train was late last night, the lights were sliding
Down off the hump when I climbed into my bed."

"Umphuh," was all the answering grunt. "Miss Leafy,
Take in huh coffee, kindly please. Huh paw
Done had his breakfus and run out asnoopin."

"Oh don't Miss-Leafy me!"

                    "Ain fitten I doan."

"But what do you call Alicia Ditmar, Thedus?"

"Ain call huh nothin, chile, jus fetch a muhmuh."

Leafy's end of their laughter ran to silence
When from the kitchen door she saw that lady,
Saw the back of a shiny head with curls
Riding in rolls… something like eggwhite frothed
The thing she wore   strange in a rough cabin
No kin to the gooseflesh showing on her arms.

She sat unthawed at a tray before the fireplace.
"Oh goodmorning," she said to the air, spoke iced and tiny.
"Is it always so bleak, October in your mountains?
You'll find a wrap on my bed; please bring it to me."

Leafy wavered, holding the tin coffeepot.
Should you pour   should you clap down the pot and run
pour out and walk, and God hold up your head
Step to that bedroom door   close it soft
Stop in front of her glass and get your trailmarks
Thanks be to God no gooseflesh rising on you
Is a voice like the lace of frost on watergrass
Going to raise the hackles along your spine
As if you were a shedog scenting a vixen
Looks like your pop was right that said more things
Hid out in just a week   Her things are lovely
Silver and silk   and would this white be ivory
Where's his picture   in a locket likely
Under her breast

         Come steady girl   come steady
Lay this furry thing along your arm
Must be a thousand skins of trapped grey squirrel
Scuttle, you lady's maid

           Oh   he is with her
Too tall to stoop for kisses   Drop the squirrels
Walk proud   walk slow   walk away to Thedus

                                                            "Leafy,"
He said, "Now stay your flying foot to meet
Alicia."

        His honeywords   the like
You never knew could be

                        "Leafy," he said,
"And what a name of sortilege you carry!
Visit my ugly fowl with us this evening
And bring her luck to lay her golden eggs."

"Good land," said Leafy, "if you mean the boat,
I'd never dare to set my foot on it.
Our boys are jealous, they say a woman brings
Bad luck to a boat. They're jealous as us, Miss Ditmar,
Would you want a man to go plunging around your kitchen?"

Alicia glanced at her own rose-varnished fingers.
"I couldn't even imagine it," she breathed coolly.

Never watched her own bread brown in her oven
Thought Leafy.

[Olsen]

*Tensions mount: Alicia is displeased that John has invited
a serving girl to see the dredging, and dismisses his defense
of how things are done in "mountain country." Meanwhile,
the goldboat's less-than-solid construction has started
making problems for the dredging operation. Consequently,
MacWhirter does not operate the machine aggressively enough
for Ditmar's liking.*

Ditmar faced him full. "You mean to tell me
You're not at bedrock yet? You've had no cleanup?"

"No cleanup and no chance of it…"

"Good God, man,
Do you think it's a baby incubator you're running?
Do you think we're made of money, to rebuild
Before we show a profit? Push her harder?
We've got to get results."

No trouble hearing
The metal of that voice, that engine racing.
How to answer an engine   how to render
The days   the nights   with your heart in your mouth
    burning
Every time she dug on a rock   every time
The bucketline jerked back

Here was the chasm
Here it opened   divided two men standing
Possessor from doer   manipulator from lover

Finally Dorn's mouth came open to answer
Unreason out of a pit unguessed, came open
But the words never got said.

That moment
Boatquake followed on soulquake. That moment
In one terrific sickening threeway jar
Shuddered an actual throe. Bodies were shaken,
Thrown against the wall. The bucketline roared,
Stopped dead. Sharp bells rang over, shouts,
Stamping of feet below, up ladders, through runways.

[...]

Alicia first   safe
Limp in her corner   green pallor round her hands
That covered eyes and mouth

The same green
On faces hung from the windows slack and staring

MacWhirter grey to his hair, hand frozen to a lever,
Croaked out of a stiff throat, "Olsen overobard."

Young Olsen   oiler   the same that would grin, "Hi boss,"
Going off shift   "Then why are you all gaping?
Get boathooks, man the rowboat."

"That's attended to."

Dorn's coat went off for a dive.

"Wait," said MacWhriter.
"Look."

He pointed. Down by the ladderlines
Between the dredge and the bank bubbled a stain.
A thing triangular, red, drifted over the sump.
One of the crew vomited into the wellshaft.

Steady   pay no heed to the cold sweat beading
Steady, the boss   "Olsen I met on deck, off shift."
Off shift   to his ridiculous baby-wife
That would sit melon-pregnant by a coffin

Faces turned from the pit, accused MacWhirter.
MacWhirter moistened his lips. "Olsen stopped,
Why, I don't know."

          "A match," said someone hoarsely.
"Borrowed a light off me. Says, 'My pipe ain't drawin.'
Hell, if he'd only went with the boys, I thought then…"

"Shut up," said MacWhirter. "A hell of a lot of difference
Now, what you thought.

          Well, three minutes, say,
And there he goes, alone on the plank, asteamin
Long about in the middle. I know I shouldn't
Accordin to rule have took an eye off of him
Till he touched ground. But hell, that very minute
She chose to let out a screech."

          His eyes turned
Basilisk on Alicia where she fought
Silent the waves of nausea.

          "And I slewed round.
Thought she was stabbed. Or maybe I didn't think.
A spider   she says.   Something about a spider.
And then the boat bucked on some friggin rock.

"God," he said, and swallowed hard. His face
That had been grey, reddened with a grim anger.

"When I turned back," he said, "it wasn't two seconds,
His arms and legs was flyin every whichway
Over the pond. He fouled the bucketline.
I have lost a life," said MacWhirter, "account of a bitch."

There came a gasp. Ditmar stood in the doorway.
"Fire that man."

               MacWhirter   the one case-hardened
Out of your whole crew   and for a word
A motion of the lips   a breath from the mouth

"Get your time," said Dorn.

               MacWhirter spoke
And his cicatrice glistened against a crimson cheek.
"Ain't no buzzard can give you the order to fire me.
I quit when I spoke that word."

Telegrams [V]

*Alicia and Ditmar having gone back east, MacWhirter
leaving the dredging operation, the death of Olsen, the damage
to the boat, and the increasingly apparent unprofitability of
the operation all hit John Dorn hard. Dorn is surprised
when Ditmar sends a glowing report on the operation to the
stockholders. Dorn objects that the facts have been exaggerated,
but Ditmar dismisses his concerns. The divide between John
and Alicia grows wider, and Ditmar rejects Dorn's estimates
for repairs to the goldboat. It is in the midst of this that the
boat is laid up for winter.*

DORN TO SUMMIT GOLD CO

Following your instructions
Dredge laid up for winter
Protest curtailment
Crew of two watchmen
Cannot meet emergencies

SUMMIT GOLD CO TO DORN

No emergency likely   stop
Crew deemed sufficient

DITMAR TO DORN

Stockholders restive   stop
Reorganization
Under advisement   stop
Come east vacation
All expenses paid

DORN TO DITMAR

Dare not leave dredge
In crippled condition

Strongly opposed
Change of organization
During present crisis

DITMAR TO DORN

Change customary
Under such conditions
Recapitalization
Now deemed imperative.

DORN TO DITMAR

Strongly opposed
If shareholders suffer

DITMAR TO DORN

Leave these policies
To my expertise   stop
I take care of your interests   stop

Alicia impatient

ALICIA TO JOHN

Come be my valentine

JOHN TO ALICIA

Loved I not honor

ALICIA TO JOHN

Then never come

It was a frozen day of tough midwinter
That Dorn and Buffin came to the icelocked boat
Halfhearted measuring for meager repairs.
The peaks wore rags of cloud, a diamond breath
Moved steady from the north to frost their nostrils,
And leafed as it passed the sheaf of yellow papers
Dorn read aloud. His voice rose on the last:
I take care your interests. He snorted, rocked
Hard on the balls of his feet.

          "Is that," he said,
"A thing to say in answer to my protests?"

Buffin looked at him. What was this naked baby
Doing among the cougars? "You hold stock?"

"Why yes, of course that's in my contract. Yes."

"Then the old skunk, I have to beg your pardon,
Old Ditmar means that he'll transfer your stock
Without you losin nothin. He somehow don't figure
On lettin his manager down."

          "But man, the others,
The schoolteachers, the farmers, all the plain people!"

"Can roll a hoop to hell."

          A stormy silence
Fell on the frozen deck.

          "In that case, Buffin,
He is a skunk."

          "Well, not for me to say to you."

[The nightwatchman]

The winter sets in, but Ike Buffin predicts a thaw and warns
Dorn to take more precautions with the integrity of the boat.

Chinook blew up too warm from the northwest,
Steely blasts from the East charged over the wires,
And at dead center whirled a secret eddy
To wreak disaster.

        Hicks nightwatchman, chosen
For being steady and busy-handed, boat-minded,
Took right away to gnawing at his nails.
Hicks was that kind of nervy little man
That twitched if he hadn't something in his hands
Such as an ax or a rope or his woman's body.
Couldn't just sit and let the hours go over
And doze between rounds among flickering shadows
Under the hulks of motionless machinery
That didn't have to be oiled or wiped or fiddled with.
There was only the pump engine to keep under steam.
You got that tended to and then where were you?

A man could go bats in no time watching the clock.
Look forward to the round like it was heaven,
And what a goddam treat when it come off!
Nine minutes to tromp round in her mouldy bowels,
Nine more for the decks, and nothing there
Only the sky and the ice and this damn chinook
That pushed up to you like a woman…

        The second night
He stopped at the liquor store and bought him a pint,
Nursed it along to four o'clock, rode easy,
Coasted home on top of the world. Next night
Made it a custom. It would tide him over
Till a man could blaze his trail.

On that soft evening
When the chinook's last losening held mercury
Three hours from sunset above freezing point,
Hicks stepped the early stage of just a pint
Up to a quart. His pint hadn't turned the trick
The night before, ran out when he wasn't noticing.
Along about half-past four it had soured on him,
Nothing you could put your finger on to remember.
Nothing, snaking up on you out of nowhere.
Plenty tonight to see him through and one
To grow on.

An inch of water top of the ice
When he took over at seven, and everything tidy.
Nothing to bother a man with a quiet bottle
Till seven morning, only to make the rounds
And keep some pressure showing in the gauge.

He made the eight-o'-clock, lurching once or twice.
There was a gurgle somewhere, and what of it
Have a little drink   No need at all
To be stingy with your drinks   a stingy guy
Was no damn good   he stank   Stank, that was it

With my foot in the stirrup and my ass in the saddle
I'm aridin around behind this goddam cattle
Singing oo-ooley oo...

Full bellying
The song rang round the cavern, rose and bawled.
Later it fell. Slowly steam in the gauge
Showed low, showed lower, lowest. A long snore
Hailed time for the next round.

[The Goldboat settles]

*Dorn, aware that Hicks has allowed the boat's pump to fail,
comes aboard the goldboat to inspect it and to write Alicia
a letter from a secluded place. While he is aboard, the boat
begins to sink from the water it has taken on during the thaw.
In this excerpt, Dorn tries to climb out of the sinking boat
while looking for the nightwatchman, whom he assumes has
drowned.*

                                    That moment
Hell let loose with a roar. The pond rose up
In one big wave. There was a sound of splitting.
All of a sudden out of nowhere canted
The forward gantry to lean above his face,
Blacking out the stars.

                    Cold sweat broke out
Over his belly.

               Down by the bow   Dorn
Inside   in the black water

                     Go it careful
One step wrong, the whole caboodle goes
And the old bitch has three to her credit

                       First
The guiderope   there, under our hand   now
Feel for the plank   Jesus what an angle
Down into the dark   claw down   down
Maybe next step your foot'll be in water
What's that noise ahead   like wood chattering
Onto wood   why that might be the plank
Hitting against the housing   busted loose
Some chance then

                    Guiderope gone away
Let your legs down either side of the plank
In ache of water   hitch along on your hams
Housing overhead now   here's a hole
In black   must be on the upper deck

Lucky, the winchhouse door   if you
Reach up and chin yourself   and hold   hard
Made it, by God!

                    Trembling all over   now
Squat down   study the next move

                                        When Dorn
Came to the deck he felt the push of water
Running over his feet. Instinctively
He grasped at the first support that came to hand,
The forward stairway rail. The shock fell
On a brain like a rag frozen. The overheaving
Terrible crash and tremor of the dredge,
The swirl of water up the cavern, up
Against his body, pinned him to the wall.
Water receded, slapped, slapped again higher.

Something in him came aware enough
To fight the tide. His hands began to edge
Along that madly angled rail. Water flowed
Below his chin, space of air grew smaller
Over his head. Getting dizzy   can't
Edge up much farther   MacWhirter used to call
Having that rail a tenderfoot trick

                                hang to it
A minute longer

     Captain went down with his boat
With all the river running through his boat

Is this God's iron grip under your arm

Easy does it, have you out of this
If the goddam boathook holds and your arm don't break

Easy easy now

     A long while after
Leaning against the slope of the winchhouse wall
He heard Ike Buffin's voice go gruffly past him
Speaking as to a dear foolhardy son
In proud relief and fury. "Seen his track,
The bugger, plain as the slot of a snowshoe rabbit
Pointed out to his getaway, knowed then
There you was, ariskin your life for a bastard."

Dorn staggered up. He felt outrageous laughter
Climb through an empty pit into his gullet,
Threw back his head and let it have its way
Above the river running through his boat.

"Buffin," he gasped, rocking between the hoots
"Here stands before you God's sorest tenderfoot."

Telegrams [VI]
This section immediately follows the previous.

DORN TO DITMAR

Dredge sank last night
Resting on two sandbars
Leaks sprung in hull
Just about waterline
Melted out in thaw
Only one watchman
Pursuant to your orders
Your guarantee imperative
Expense of raising dredge
Watchman skipped country

SUMMIT GOLD CO
TO JOHN DORN MGR

Hold you responsible
Any damage done   stop
Find expense of raising
Out of your own pocket

JOHN DORN
TO SUMMIT GOLD CO

Your board responsible
Insufficient funds
Inadequate crew
Cause of disaster
Gross injustice
Done to my managership

DITMAR TO DORN

Code	Translation
oeillade	I expect
burgonet	you
paragoge	to keep
lotophagi	cool
coparcenary	sell
espartito	shares
almandine	ten dollars
estacade	per share
thor	lose no time
mezuzah	confidential

DITMAR TO DORN

thor	lose no time
coparcenary	sell
espartito	shares
purbash	before
peridot	bankruptcy
Answer my telegrams	

[Dorn resigns/Conclusion]

Disillusioned by the behavior of Ditmar and the board, Dorn
dreams of the goldboat he had envisioned, carefully contructed
and intelligently run—the operation which would win him
the respect of his boss and the affection of his sweetheart.
He consults with Thedus, who reads the tarot for him and
warns him that his desires can come from a gate of gold or
a gate of horn, but only he knows which is which. He leaves
to contemplate this, and passes along the same roads that he
had galloped down upon his arrival to Rockinghorse, when his
future had been a brighter affair.

This was the road to his goldboat   this was the road
A boy had charged along   up through the valley
To burst the mountains open

                    Mountains resist
You stand a man against them   they'll not rot you
As soon as look at you

                    The fugue of ranges
Swung strongly under space and marched in rhythm
Rooted and greatly soaring. Now more sharp
Than any word can tell it, irrevocable
The undivided moment came. He passed
That moment through the horny gate.

                    Dorn's telegram,
The last that was wrung from him, was handed in
By Dorn in person to the station agent
Ten minutes later:

            Accept my resignation
Send new manager

At the ticket window
As he cast that seed behind him and went out,
Burst up a flower of joy. "Guts," said the agent,
"He's got the guts of Jesus." His poker face
Broke up in filaments of glee. He rose
Ponderous from his stool and stood in the doorway
To observe the back of an honest-to-God he-horse
Go loping down the street.

      Dorn didn't guess
The warmth that rose behind him. All he knew
Was a hot thrust and clamor in his body
Now to move clean in space, and not afraid,
And not alone.

     And so he came to the cabin,
Was out of his straps and in at the door before Leafy
Had more than time to take her hands from her bread-dough.
She saw his face passionate, clear. Her knees smote
Sweetly, knowing her hour came. Home about her
Went his arms, and hers about his shoulders
And the breath went out of them both.

       A long time after,
"Leafy," he said, "Leafy teach me soon
The way I am to live. The gate is horny
Into mountain country.

     Leafy," he said,
"How shall I wait, how shall I wait for you?"

She looked at him in strength and gentleness.
"My love," she said, "my child, no need to wait.
I am your woman."

FROM **THE TENMILE RANGE** (1957)

The mountains over Breckenridge, Colorado (c. 1957)

THE TENMILE RANGE

Foreword

Needs must harry the Tenmile now:
Hot in the channels behind the bone
The words are up and the drum beats over,
The drum beats over, the words must go.

Never along that range is ease:
Things are warped that are too near heaven,
Ink runs clotted down the pen,
Verse has the twist of timberline trees.

Topography

The Great Divide is a full-sprung bow
About that country, and its arrow
Is the length of the Tenmile, notch to tip.
Stark is the streamhead where the narrow
Careless snowrills stop and go,
Atlantic, Pacific, freeze or flow.

Weather Conditions

Never along that range is ease:
The rose of the winds goes wheeling over,
When there is peace and little woe
Dust devils rise and blow
Sucking the air from the river valley.
Water and blood will boil too early,
Atoms cry for their release.

Government

Set in dominion over these
None has ruled them since the flow
That set their homestead solitaires
And spattered wire-gold filigrees.
Magistrate and forester
Exist forlorn in those rude airs
Where dwell the ancient liberties.

History

There was meat and miniver,
Buckskin and beaver fur.
When these had strained away
Goldflake sifted from the poke.
Twice raped and rough with scars
Freehold, gone lean and grey,
Stands at the end of wars.

Time as a Well-Spring

I thought, said Mr. Probus, there was time,
Time by the dipperful, time lipping, flowing
Out of some plenteous spring where I'd be going
With my bright dipper, frosting it with rime,
Hoarding no more than God would hoard a dime,
Slipping time over my palate, careless blowing
Drops off my moustache, wasting it full knowing
There would be more, more always, soft and prime.

I've lived some years at Stringtown, Probus said,
Back in the mountain mining molybdenum,
Gassed and sent in again and lined with lead.
Seven years some few will last who stand the gaff.
Sometimes where the machines bore, springs will come.
I have to laugh, he said, I have to laugh.

Lunch Time in the Tunnel

I have my castle, Probus said, and when
I shall have done with this godawful hole,
Broken my pick and shinnied up the pole,
I shall go forth and view its spires again.
And I shall hit the trail across Peak Ten
And down along the river air my soul
Till pinned to heaven itself pricks up the goal
With the brown cabin under, Probus-den.

So man the pumps, he said, and tallyho,
Heave up the anchor, gentlemen, for now
We move to disembogue the old she-cow,
The gangrened guts of Satan's so-and-so.
Judas arch hellion intercede for us
Who ditch our dreams to muck out Erebus.

Lyric Mood

Nan, Mr Probus said, you want a spring
Right in your room to cool your young hot breast
And wash your mouth that mouths like mine have pressed
With clean wild water for the bright blood-sting
On your rose-tallowed lips. My sullied wing,
My overlaid, my thumb-worn palimpsest,
I'll choose the iced, the prime, the liveliest
From my blue valley for your sweetening.

Have your lips known a spring, he said, your feet
A spring? We've hot and cold, she said: you know
Miss Mae don't let we girls go off the Street
Dabbling around in springs. You old sourdough,
Where is this place you wash your feet in, dear?
Away from here, he sighed. Away from here.

Hardrock Miner

Mountains were made for badgers, Probus said,
And badgers for the mountains. And so long
As I can claw a tunnel, with the strong
Smell of the ore beyond, I shall be led
To sink my pick in holes unlimited,
To rummage in old stopes and raise the song
Of victory too soon, all laid along
Hellbent to crack a granite maidenhead.

And men-of-war may hoot and presidents
Rock down the chutes to hell, but I'll be going
Soon as a patch of mountainside is showing.
Soon as a bluebird settles on a fence,
Two shall string out and beat it up the trail,
A jackass first, a miner at his tail.

Mountain Woman

God love these mountain women anyway,
Said Mr Probus. Not to say they're fair
Or sleek with oils, for woodsmoke in the hair
And sagebrush on the fingers every day
Are toughening perfumes, and the sunstreams flay
Too dainty flesh. But what remains is rare,
Like mountain honey to the mountain bear.
He finds his relish in a rough bouquet.

Days when their wash is drying, off they'll go
And fish the beaver ponds. Hell or high water
They'll wade the slues in sunburnt calico
Playing a trout like some old sea-king's daughter.
Hell and high water women… Steady now,
Not all of them, he said. One, anyhow.

Address to a Tenderfoot

So your belief is that peace is found,
Said Mr Probus, resident in hills,
That mountain towns are loaded to the gills
And oiled with peace, that pine mat on the ground
Was cushioned there for comfort to abound.
Wait till the trails are iced, till winter fills
These bowls with silence, till abandoned mills
Crack knuckles and it snows until you're drowned.

Then fools are blown to hell in some white welter,
Brushed with the snowsmoke off a streaming ledge,
Ripped open on a jagtooth's outer edge.
Then wise men tough the winter out in shelter,
Melt down their fat like bears in hollow trees.
Well, call it peace, he said, if you so please.

Miner's Pension

This dalliance with heaven on a hill,
Said Mr Probus, smudges out the dream,
This land whose powdered milk I disesteem,
Whose drop of honey figures in the bill,
Whose angels monthly swarm past Probus-sill
Setting their feathers in a gentle steam
To flutter queries that a jay might deem
Too rowdy for his modesty to spill.

Yet I that had my dreamings otherwise,
That fought the rock and lost, and always lost,
Have on this hill my freehold and my skies:
My hot he-den against the winter frost,
All space to howl through when my mood is so,
All stars to rock with at my own fool show.

Opus 8

Our god was ice with goldleaf plastered on:
We built his boats that dredged for his veneer,
Gutted our valleys to his lordly blare
Of loud expensive laughter and bon ton.
Under our icefields standing to the sun
We watched him match the glitter of their dare,
And stamp his stallions down that brittle air,
Proud in our sight and peerless in his own.

He died, said Probus, melted down and died
And never heard the coyotes take his hill,
Passed in reeks of incense undenied.
Now all he was has assayed out to nil,
And newer outfits sweating hope and blood
Raise in his place yet more preposterous gods.

Summons to the Undertaker

If it's pneumonia, Mr Probus said,
Don't skid me off the Tenmile or I'll haunt
Your genteel casketry, old cormorant,
Old chronic end of evening. Dig my bed
Right in the boneyard at the valleyhead.
You never caught them dodging from their gaunt
Uncompromising deaths. I seem to want
To join the firstfruits on the watershed.

You'll find the makings of a poker party
Inside my cady. Play the snorting mule,
The she-mule of my luck .. A mining fool
Deserves a rough-box .. Play her tough and hearty,
Oldtimer, fan her till her ears are bent.
And if she runs, erect my monument.

from HOUSE IN THE VALLEY

Walls

The logs have been sealed away and overlaid
Paper on paper. You long to peel the stuff,
The flowered, the plain, the dearbought dim brocade,
Down to the muslin, down to the old buff,
Down to whatever is left of a man dead,
A bit of wool maybe dyed with butternut
Caught in the mitered corner, a hair of him shed,
Or sweet in the wood the name of a girl cut.
There's not a man or a ledger to tell his name
Or whether he hewed from lodgepole or spruce or fir,
But wherever his bones are on the range or the plain
Here in old years his bones and his brains were.
Every time a nail strikes into the chinking,
Into the hollow of time, it will set you thinking.

Window on the Range

Intolerable the marching of this range,
This fugue of sight unbroken and immense,
In theme and counterpoint forever strange,
Forever overflowing human sense.
Impose upon your lips the native game
Of undertruth, the minimum of awe:
At sunset when the snowsmoke drifts in flame
Say it is pretty, presently withdraw
From stern crescendos rising overlong.
And though the drive and rhythm of that ramp
Runs endless eastward resonant and strong,
Pull down the curtain, sit beside the lamp
Until the world within your eyeballs' arc
Rocks to its poise against the rushing dark.

Dialog

Let's step outside in the mountain night, renew
Whole vision of this integer of cells:
This house, in separate amber shining so,
Uniquely seen, as though another self:
Unit in space, now for a time clearly
Walled, roofed, warmed: now for a time...
How little, how long? Whisper it flawless, dare we?
Shout it, and count the neighbor rays that shine,
Digits of oneness, careless into space...
Yet if tomorrow, yet if tomorrow shaken,
Lightless, forlorn?
                    Therefore. Look, while the eyes
Know this for ours, and the amber word still spoken.
Though wood shall rot and light shatter, though
Self dissolve on a breath, this house is now.

In Those Rude Airs

Mayflower gulch is deep, is still.
Over its walls the range winds toss,
But never a buckbush stirs below
Where rills go stealthy under moss.

All winter silence breeds and grows
Out of that wildness and that frost.
Wolverines move ruthless there,
Wildcats too, but men the most.

Two partners trap in Mayflower,
Red and Whitey, secret men.
There are few words between those two
More than would pass in a he-bears' den.

Red snared a bride at Kokomo,
Baited her with a cross-fox skin,
Wrapped it around her pretty neck,
Loaded his sled and pulled her in.

Her eyes were slant, her tongue was slim,
A cat's tongue for a massacre.
Folk at Kokomo prophesied
Whitey would lose the field to her.

The Sagehen shook a claw at that
(She birthed you and she buried you),
Said: She will be the hell and gone
Before she parts them old gumshoes.

Well, winter drew to March, to March
When trails are iced and atoms crackle,
And shacks will choke with straw on straw,
And each new straw an itch to battle.

The end of March in Kokomo
And every drift a honeycomb,
Over the trail from Mayflower
A man was seen to slip and come.

He slips and comes to Sagehen's door
That hour when cabin-smoke begins.
Through frosted cracks the whispers fly:
A laying-out or lying-in.

Under the sawteeth shot with pink
Hovers a town on bated breath:
It's Whitey. What if a kid's been slipped?
What if a death, what if a death?

The long white hours had spun to dusk
When back toward home the Sagehen sped,
And two behind her slewing wide
To the balk and lunge of a loaded sled.

And a door slams, and nothing more
Till at last the emptied sled is gone,
Till the light that never dies from snow
Etches a crony keeping on,

THE UNSUNG MASTERS SERIES

Creeping on and entering
Where the Sagehen sits to toast her bones.
The fat jug gurgles for a brew
And breath comes thick with overtones.

Three hot ones and the breath steams loose
And the tongue leaps without a rein:
He said she'd a yen for rabbit stew,
Tripped on a root and blew her brains.

Twenty below at dawn, if one;
Her blood had froze her to that door
She laid on ... Now I ask of you,
What did she hunt in slippers for?

Mayflower gulch is deep, is still,
Is furred in wordlessness and frost.
Wolverines move ruthless there,
Weasels too, and men the most.

Words About a Place

The tail of your eye, your nostrils know the ombre
Of what was here. You know a stand of timber,
Stout, having purple cones ambered with resin
That roared along this chimney. And you know
The smell of gold in a hole, perverse and somber.

Five hewn logs bedded in moss and mallow,
A pride of spruces in an unroofed still-house
Under a three-faced peak; a name on granite,
A scrap or two from the junk of a man's head,
And into the tail of your eye comes up the shadow.

But the words have not come up, they have not found you,
For a town blanched at the head of a high valley,
For what was first out of the turf returning,
Out of the springs, out of the strong rock,
Never the words, only the air thinned round you.

Belle Turnbull by the stove (c. 1957)

High Trail

The trail is
thin   dear
loneliest
the one road
vein-strait
the one road
wheel-clear
foot-wise
celibate
thin   dear
the trail is

Observations Above Timberline

How am I to tell you?
I saw a bluebird
a bluebird incandescent
flying up the pass

and where the wind came over
the Great Divide came over
invisible and mighty
he struck a wall of glass.

I saw his bright wings churning
I saw him stand in heaven
the bird's power   the wind's power
miraculously hold—

Now I will tell you
dare my soul to say it
speak the name of beauty
accurate and cold.

Short Lease

Out in the willows
was our spring
cold   clear
flowing away.
Late in the fall
Annie would say
Two little trout,
just two,
will come to your spring.

Late in the autumn
this came true:
In a snow ring
the water lay
cold   clear
flowing away:
Two little trout
knife-blue
swam in our spring.

Long Lease

For since a rock's a long, long treasure:
a rock, a root, a south exposure:
the loan of these is our forever.

To Be Tacked on a Cabin Door

From everlasting space
my roof shall fold you
my bed's spare privacy
restore, remold you
my hearth's dispassionate eye
alone behold you.

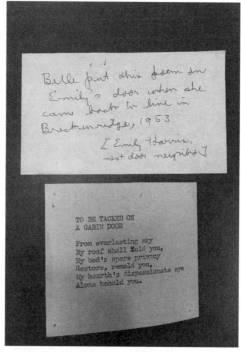

The handwritten explanatory card reads:
"Belle put this poem on Emily's door when she
came back to live in Breckenridge, 1953.
        "(Emily Harris, next door neighbor)"

Pasque Flowers

The earth's in cataclysm
storm-bound, deprived of Heaven:
Yet round the wasteland these
punctual presences
stand up in amethyst
mist-whorled, unearthliest:
Deep-footed against death
springs the returning wreath.

Cycle: I. Sun Dance

Eastward the cliff's
terrible wing is
westward the mountain
Slowly the drums
low and portentous
deepen their throbbing
till the air quivers
till the air pulses
hums as a drumhead
till the heart swells
shaken and lonely
Under a cliff's wing
bronze are the dancers
buckskin and feather
wampum and silver
leap to the drumbeat
faster oh higher
stronger the dancers
take on their eyeballs
the God in his sunburst
turn as the sunflower
under his triumph
over the rock
over the juniper
over the mountain

Cycle: II. Easter Service

Eastward the cliff's
terrible wing is:
westward the moutain.
Furred in the dawnspring gather the people
shivering, murmuring, herded quiescent:
hark to the choir, to the Evangel
to the bright bells on the wave-length appointed:
trumpet-led to the heavenly vision
take on their shielding eyelids to the sunburst:
trundle away, away to their breakfasts.
Slowly the red dust, the
scrapings of ages
over the junipers
billows and settles.

Bomber Over Breckenridge

Lie still: not here the crater heaves,
not here the hot stars shock and burst:
Tune clangor out to silence, listen
to the slow hum of quiet loves

which muted couch in moss. Lie still,
drowse under sun. Whittle your bed,
your rooftree down, pile ranges round you,
crevasse, impasse, unfathomed bowl—

Lie still, drink at the thin springs
and mark dim woodbirds where they fly
the farther side—The farther side?
yet in the air what gong begins?

what desperate great gong begins
over the roofs and the cupola?
Oh glorious, malignant Oh,
Hell's dearest bird is on the wing.

These Who Shorn Return

Those years there was the wind, always the wind
raking our peaks whence help, it is said, cometh:
savaging the undersides of birds,
tearing at trees, chocking the cabin-breath
down again in our chimneys: Those were the years
everything that was fastened came unhinged:

Boys kept blowing away, do you remember?
Live hair stood in the wind, in the wind rushing,
young fingers made the V in a blur of trumpets—
These who shorn return, whose drifting eyes
lift to our peaks whence help (it is said) cometh
mark there the sign inverse, the edged reminder.

By Stravinsky

Up sprang from peace, from peace, that naive bride:
Marched in a wind of drums, unsatisfied:
Where a drum smote too deep, bled died—
At star-shriek rose again, Death's horns astride.

Never the Words (A MONOLOG)

Needs must go prowling timberline over and over
tossing the feckless words aside in windows:

Brush off that guff about conies that flick and vanish,
kiss away this finial one-flower gentian
whose cool blue syllable will melt in the fingers:

So is it that cover begins where nakedness wavers?
or is it that candor ends where cover lingers?

Blow off that echo-noise, all that fluff, perpend:

Then since the whole is the sum of its so-and-sos,
why not work up the honey-flowers of this tundra
upcurved to besiege its boulders, this crevice cloven
by the magenta horns of its saxifrage, why not
filch (façon de parler) these aloof, these insulate
huddles of fir, these enclaves, ah, enclave, ah,
what a lov-e-ly word! better try it, what?

God, no! dig, for the truth lies under, somewhere
under:
    Now this:
               this maybe?
                         maybe:
Timberline is the utmost stop of timber.

So what remains to be said? the i's are dotted.

UNCOLLECTED & UNPUBLISHED POEMS

Belle Turnbull and Helen Rich (left) at the 9 French Street cabin they shared.

Sonnet to Gertrude Buck

It fell that turning of a page I came
Upon the great clear shining of your face,—
Your face, that like a calm, unwavering flame
Burns yet before me in this far-off place.
The same deep-seeing eyes beneath the white
Broad forehead, with its quiet wings of hair;
The sweeping classic of the nose; the might
And sweetness of your mobile mouth were there.
How many women, poring on that page,
Remembering how fine you were, how true,
Have thrilled exultant in their heritage,
Proud that you lived, and that they share in you.
How many women, softly, as they read,
Have bowed themselves and wept that you are dead.

Song for Female Voices

Ladies, keep your strangeness:
At the dusk
Wear it as a mantle,
Subtly fragrant—
Not with lilies,
Not with musk...

Ladies, keep your strangeness—
In the dark
Veil on veil flung round you,
Lest the starlight,
Lest the moonlight
Show you stark.

Ladies, keep your strangeness,
And at dawn,
Wrapped and hooded in it—
Not with weeping,
Not with singing—
Oh, be gone!

Mountain-Mad

Mountains cast spells on me—
  Why, because of the way
Earth-heaps lie, should I be
Choked by joy mysteriously;
  Stilled or drunken-gay?

Why should a brown hill-trail
  Tug at my feet to go?
Why should a boggy swale
Tune my heart to a nameless tale
  Mountain marshes know?

Timberline, and the trees
  Wind-whipped, and the sand between—
Why am I mad for these?
What dim thirst do they appease?
  What filmed sense brush clean?

Reckoning

HERS

There yet remains the evening of this day...
    Far off the clamor of the hurrying train
Roars up against the canyon and away,
    Leaving me void and effortless and slain.
There yet remain the mountain and the moon,
    Too surely poised, too splendidly austere:
They do not care that all my senses swoon—
    My veins run white—because of you, my dear.

I wish that like some little furry beast,
    That yearns and mates and straight is whole again,
I might stand free of memory and, released,
    Be spared this sick unrest, this after-pain—
What am I saying? I will pay—will pay—
Oh, gladly!—for the morning of this day!

HIS

Noon on the shuttling, many-clanking street:
    Hot breath of asphalt where the pavements glare;
    Foul breath of jockeying autos everywhere...
What is that sudden whiff, pervasive, sweet—
Stinging my jaded pulses' slogging beat—
    Of juniper and balsam on the air?
    Close to the curbing shrinks a rancher's mare,
Drawing a load of pine that fries with heat...

I could forget my manhood; I could lean
    My head upon that wretched cart and cry
For that brown girl I loved among the clean
    Crushed balsam boughs, whose fragrance, hot and dry,
Filled earth and heaven and all that lay between—
    Pine-breath will be her incense till I die!

FROM THE LONG ARC

The Answer's in the Back

Circumscribe however well
your sector geometrical
upon the earth's reluctant sphere
still it will be haunted, shared,
skewed, bulged here and there,
spun along a vast ellipse:
earth-pulled   sun-hurled
star-tugged   moon-twitched
petal-flung by that and this—

Relax says the psychiatrist.

[Weather Report]

Leda bedded with a swan:
Danae with gold was won:
Europa rode upon a bull,
For Jove was always fanciful.
Now the myth is down upside:
Wafts of silver iodide
out of a plane assume the god
to get with rain a maiden cloud.

This Fir

Is a fir noble? is a fir
jade-springing? *Is* a fir?
Wind, hail upon it, sun
upon it: to know sun upon
this fir-tree, in the looping brain
what flashes, what vibrations running
cell to cell, and beauty born
that moment out of a glue of matter
on rod and cone hung upside down! Then
when rod and cone and brain are gone
and the last poem blown nowhere
is a fir not, with none to care?

Now the Slow Dawn

                    relentless along the prairie
dredges unready men out of the pits of sleep:
Untwine your heart from the dream, rise, go out to the dairy:
go out to the north-mowing; surely the dream will keep.

Epitaph for Clelia, a Spinster

Pity her not so smugly,
mesdames, messires:
Marrow of dreams sustained her
small-bosomed years:
For women dead of surfeit
reserve your tears.

The Long Arc

Plagued by each cactus stumbled on
Sybilla stony in her chair:
Drank of silence till her tongue
soundless belled upon the air:
The arc swings out, the arc swings down.
Little else is shown, child:
This is shown.

No Other Water

Timberline folk think small of edges,
by cosmic thunders are lulled to rest,
whether they come from shaft or schoolhouse
are intimate with a mountainhead:
Theirs are the naked, the wind-swept ridges,
theirs the springs at the watershed.

Lou, Mrs. Willow said, knew no other water—
And sweet? she was sweet as water from our spring:
Lovely she was, my honey-color daughter,
boys and hummingbirds courted her.
So what must she choose for mate of her Junetime?
what but a dryfarm cockleburr...

Far as forever lay she in deathbed,
down off our basin, out and again;
far as his windmill, caked at the wellhead,
limed with the water that leached her veins—
Tell me no other, the balsam I brought her
died by her grave, *Oh God*, the same.

Small Stone

Had done with trinkets, cherished a small stone
out of some channel pounded by the rain:
bedded it in an ark of porcelain
where caracoled in a medallion
a feather-toed insoucient griffon:
Had pleasure in that delicate design
to hoard a downright solid of the prime
inside a composition so mondaine:

Eyed it not seldom in that tenement,
drew toward it home from each hot journeying:
one could not lay a cheek to anything
more clean, more cool, more webless of intent.
Spoke once into the final graceless hour:
Give me the stone; I will not hold your flower.

Inward Tussle for a Couple of Lines

Now let's not go prowling timberline for words:
it isn't only these conies that flick and vanish,
it isn't even this final one-flower gentian
whose cool blue syllable will melt in the fingers...

Then is it that cover begins where nakedness ends?
or is it that candor ends where cover begins?

What fluff!   be still now . Wait, perpend ...

OK... But since the whole is the sum of its you-know-whats
why not use the honey-sweets of this tundra
upcurved to besiege its boulders, this crevice cloven
by the magenta tongues of its saxifrage? why not
circle (façon de parler) this aloof, this insulate
huddle of surly firs, this enclave? Say, *enclave*,
what a word! why not use it, shall we?

We shall not. We shall dig harder, dig under ...

NOW :

Timberline is earth's one lone, one scraggly
ultimate name for the utmost stop of timber.

Never the Words (A MONOLOG) [variant]

Needs must go prowling timberline over and over
tossing the feckless words aside in windrows—
Brush off that guff about conies that flick and vanish,
kiss away this finial one-flower gentian
whose cool blue syllable melts in your fingers

*

Well, is it that cover begins where nakedness wavers—
or is it that candor ends where cover lingers?
Blow off that fluff and that rhyme-noise and perpend—

**

Then since the whole is the sum of its so-and-sos
why not work in the honey-flowers of this tundra
upcurved to besiege its boulders, this crevice cloven
by the magenta horns of its saxifrage—why not
filch (façon de parler) these aloof, these insulate
huddles of fir, these enclaves—ah, enclave, ah,
what a lov-e-ly word! better try it, ha, shall we?
God, no! dig, for the truth lies under, somewhere
under—

***

      Now this—
            this maybe—
                    Dare it!
Timberline is the one, the umbilical, the
ultimate word for the upmost stop of timber.

UNPUBLISHED MISCELLANY

Delinquent Tax List of Summit County

Only greyheads, pinched and few,
High up the Valley of the Blue,
Mumble the names that all men knew.

The Fisherman Mill, the Orthodox,
The Silver Eel, the Prize Box...

Gold boats munching up the Swan,
Digging the pits they floated on,
Virgin zinc in the Wellington—

The Wire-Patch, the Ontario,
The Royal Tiger, the Buffalo...

Glory holes in Farncomb Hill,
Syenite, quartzite, porphyry sill,
Level to level, of mine and mill—

The Silver Wedge, the Iron Edge,
The Rose, the Rose of Breckenridge...

Zinc, lead, silver, gold,
Now you're hot, and now you're cold.
Now you're cold.

Answers to a Questionnaire

I know:
I stand at center,

I know:
that until death I am, continuing
as solely, separately one,
my fingerprint, my soul-print lone,
unduplicated anywhere.

I know
what a chord is, what's a poem
only as welded into me.

I know
my definite beginning and
my definite end.

What is your religion?

To tend my house, my body, and my spirit:
this is beauty.
To live as best I may with those whom my life
touches; to nourish them and to be nourished by them:
this is love
to contemplate, to search, compare, to winnow:
this is wisdom.

The cabin at 9 French Street (c. 1959)

Chant

Now at last I have eaten
that dark and pungent honey
which is distilled
out of blue-black monkshood,
marsh-child of forbidden beauty
together with sky-bright mertensia
dwarf-born on the high mountains
and too sweet—
Now at last have I eaten
and am consumed.

Echo

Once
across the black marsh-country
measureless between death and burial
swung your unconquered voice
tolling my name.

Stone

I choose this lichened granite
for your grave-stone:
It has forgotten
one who leaned for a while against it:
I
remember.

Deep Music

Tonight thinking of your hands
whose touch was deep music
I stood beside your grave
and the dark inward eye
beheld their dissolution.
Lacking your hands
I have renounced eternity.

Belle Turnbull with one of her Scotties.

AUTOBIOGRAPHICAL NOTE

Following is a brief autobiographical note Belle Turnbull wrote at the behest of Crown Publishers to accompany the 1953 publication of her novel, The Far Side of the Hill.

Born in Hamilton, New York. Came to Colorado Springs with her parents (she was an only child) when a child. Her father, George Turnbull, was principal of the Colorado Springs High school for many years. Very much beloved. Both father and mother dead. Belle graduated from CSHS.

Educated thereafter at Vassar. Taught five years in upstate New York, then returned to Colorado Springs to teach in the High school. When she retired she had been head of the English department for several years.

In 1938 she pulled up stakes and moved to the high mountains where she had always wanted to live. Rash, maybe, considering she was no longer young and was in uncertain health. (She is still frail-looking, but has turned out to have about the same toughness as a timberline tree.) She lives in Breckenridge, a hard-rock mining camp of less than 300, altitude 9,579. Plenty of regional coloring. Lives in a log-sided cabin on the edge of town and has no window that does not face on peaks above timberline. Breckenridge is in Summit (literally summit) County.

Miss Turnbull has a Scottie named Libby.

Has found a Vassar education not practical for mountain living. Vassar didn't teach her to deal with frozen water-pipes, or how to break trail through a 14-inch fall of snow with webs (snowshoes), or how to get rid of packrats, or how to hang a haunch of venison, or how to cut up a jag of firewood for her Franklin stove. Vassar education has its uses, however: she can write an impassioned love letter, for example. She frequently trades this talent to a Mountain Man suitor in consideration of a thoroughly dead packrat that has been making free with her premises. After 15 yrs in the mountains she has overcome other handicaps of her education: can handle a saw and an axe with considerable skill.

Has passion for well-weathered pitch knots. Likes to send hand-picked Yule logs, all bound round with kinnikinnick[1] and juniper, to friends for Christmas.

Never cooked in her life until she retired. Now first-rate. She can start with a couple of tablespoons of meat stock and dream up a sauce fit for a gourmet. People have been known to lick their plates.

Considered behind-the-times because insists upon wood and coal range for cooking and heating. Thinks the food tastes better and it does.

The Far Side of the Hill is her first major work in prose form. She already has a national reputation as a poet (bristles when called poetess or authoress, and who can blame her?) and in addition to her long narrative poem, *Goldboat*, published in book form, her shorter works have appeared in numerous magazines, etc. She was the winner of the Harriet Monroe Memorial Prize, a coveted award made by *Poetry, the Magazine of Verse*. A collection of her poems, *The Tenmile Range* (that's the name of the range she sees from her kitchen window), about the country she now lives in, is scheduled to appear in October or November of this year. She is writing another novel: working title, *Aunt Candace's Obituary*. Still writing poetry, of course.

---

[1] [Ed.] kinnikinnick (*Arctostaphylos uva-ursi*) is an evergreen plant which produces small, tulip-like blossoms in tiny, pink clusters. Also known as Bearberry, for its edible red berries.

Says this about *The Far Side of the Hill*:

"The motivation of this book has been many years of close observation of an element of our folk-fringe, the hardrock mining folk: their attitudes and background, their speech and cadences. And my life between mountain and plain has furnished ample opportunity to understand the contrasts between their dwellers.

"Perhaps the book differs from most other works in this field in its acceptance of the realities rather than the romance in the lives of mountain people. It is a study in tensions, complicated by the struggle between a simple and a complex nature."

Her adopted county loyal to her. Everyone seems excited about the book and probably the sale will be excellent. The *Summit County Journal* is selling it: perhaps the first newspaper ever to go into the book-selling business. Fred Grantham, who owns the Dillon Drugstore, also selling it.

FROM GOLD BOATS ON THE SWAN: THE STORY OF BEN STANLEY REVETT, GOLD DREDGER

Originally published in the October, 1962, issue of Colorado
Magazine, *"Gold Boats on the Swan" demonstrates Turnbull's
rigorous research, and the provenance for several of the more
memorable episodes in her verse novel. In the interests of space,
priority is given to those sections which speak directly to Revett's
biography or contextualize various episodes in* Goldboat *and
relevant dredging practices. However, those interested in the
original will find in it not only a biography of the titular gold
dredger, but also an informative account of the economy and
praxis of gold mining as it was practiced in Colorado at the
turn of the century.*

At the time that the material for use in writing about
Revett was first examined, a number of papers were kept
for reference. Of other papers, notes were made and the papers
returned to Mrs. Melissa Hayden. At the time, since the objective
was to use the notes for background in a story, notes were made
sometimes without much attention to dates and sources, though
they were kept in chronological order by year, only.

For color and background the author is deeply indebted to
the following, not one of whom is still living in 1962: George
Robinson, dredgemaster, and later County Treasurer of Summit
County and Mayor of Breckenridge: Mrs. Melissa Hayden, widow
of Revett's secretary, and herself Clerk of the District Court for

many years: and George Robert Johnson, mining engineer, who permitted my presence on a gold dredge against the wishes of his swing shift crew, to whom a woman on board was anathema. Mr. Johnson's explanations of the operation of a gold dredge were lucid and helpful, even to a woman author.

Thanks are also due to Gordon Goodridge, who dug in the Summit County records for data on placer grounds.[1]

—AUTHOR [Belle Turnbull][2]

In the history of deep mining for gold in Colorado, Ben Stanley Revett ranks as First Gold Dredger. Not only was he the first to carry through the financing, the building, and the management of the first dredge in Colorado to dig for gold; his resourcefulness and bulldog tenacity drove him on, year after year, to finish what he had begun: to find the best possible method of driving to bedrock and to bring up the gold. And against every obstacle that gold dredging in the high Rockies presents to those who attempt it, that was what he did.

The gold was there, all right. To quote from F. L. Ransome's definitive work on the geology of the Breckenridge District: Virtually every gulch in the ... District leading down from auriferous deposits has yielded gold ... On the Swan and the French creeks thickness of gold-bearing gravel is hardly over 50 feet of bedrock."[3]

It was a long road that Revett traveled from its beginning in Asia to its end in Colorado. He was born in 1858 in Calcutta, where his father was a chaplain in the British Army in India.[4] His mother, born Isabel Bruce, was a Scotswoman, in direct line

---

[1] [Ed.] Placer mining does not involve a "mine" as it is commonly conceived, being the process of collecting gold and other precious minerals that have been deposited in stream-beds and the like. Thus, the positions from which this collection is performed (the "grounds") are as crucial to the placer miner as mountainsides are to the shaft miner. "Panning for gold," so immediately recognizable in the works of Jack London and in other Yukon stories, is a form of placer mining.

[2] [Ed.] Unless preceded by an editor's mark, all footnotes are Turnbull's. The citations and citation style are original to her essay as well.

[3] Frederick Leslie Ransome, "Geology and the Ore Deposits of the Breckenridge District, Colorado." Department of the Interior, U.S. Geological Survey, Professional Paper No. 75 (Wash: G.P.O. 1911), 9.

[4] Trevor G. Thomas, "The Revett Story," Summit County Journal, May 29, 1953.

of descent from the redoubtable Robert Bruce. His first journeys were forth and back from India to England, where, following the usual custom of English gentlefolk abroad, he was sent to school. It is probable that his vocation in life was self-chosen. He was graduated from the Royal School of Mines in London, though his choice was bitterly opposed by his music teacher, who was training his excellent tenor voice for a career in opera.[5]

[...]

His first association shown in the Revett papers was in 1889, as manager of the Twin Lakes Hydraulic Mining Syndicate, Limited, a London corporation. [...]

In the same year of 1889, Revett visited the Breckenridge District of Summit County, where the search for values had never more than hesitated since the days of the Fifty-niners, and not seldom with spectacular results.[6] It was early in the year of Revett's visit that a rich strike was made in the Ontario mine on Farncomb Hill, at mention of which even now old-timers prick up their ears. Here was a challenge to a young mining engineer of courage and imagination. Here, at bedrock must like gold in gravels yet, because of their depth, unexplored, pushed in the Glacial period from the Hill downward along old channels.

[...]

Revett's resignation from the managership of the Twin Lakes Syndicate was early in 1892, the syndicate being then in liquidation. A letter of acceptance of his resignation was dated March 8, 1893. It was signed by V. H. Smith, Liquidator, registered and addressed to Mr. B. S. Revett, Passenger, per RMS Majestic of Queentown.

TRAVELS FROM GEORGE TO ALASKA

There is nothing in the letters to indicate what was Revett's next move. Mrs. Melissa Hayden, widow of his secretary, was of the opinion that he went directly from England to inspect

---

[5] Ibid.
[6] Revett papers, 1889 ff.

placer grounds in British Columbia. But there are letters received by him during that year of 1893 and from then on, ranging from Georgia to Alaska. These letters teemed with offers to let him in on fabulous discoveries of precious metal.

Other letters received by him that year show that he had under consideration operations in certain placers around Murray, Idaho. There is no evidence to show that he became associated with these properties, one of which was named the Blossom Lake placer. Toward the end of the year he accepted managership of the Couer d'Alene placer, but for unknown reasons did not take that office.

Instead, he was for most of 1893, and for an unidentified time longer, the manager of John Campion's[7] holdings on Farncomb in the District. He also was associated with the Griffin brothers of San Francisco, Frank and Maurice, members of a prominent family of San Francisco, in two great gold mining operations, the Boss and the Wapiti. He had become friends with them on a visit to the California placer grounds. During a visit which their charming sister, Mary Griffin, made to her brothers on the Hill, Revett met her for the first time. They were married in 1898.

If Mary was a charmer, Revett, according to his Breckenridge admirers, was magnetically attractive. He was no beauty in the conventional sense; his height was five feet seven, and he was pretty nearly as wide. But like many other men of that build he carried himself with such dignity as to emphasize his importance. His face was large and nobly featured, his hair and small mustache, golden, and cut in the grand style and together with his habit of dress meticulously groomed, even in those untidy places— tunnels, shafts, dredges—where gold is hunted down. Always in such places and in cities, too, he was marked by his white Stetson, his favorite wear, except for occasions of grandeur.[8]

Among the Revett records there is an enlarged photograph of himself driving a visitor down the steep and unimproved road

---

[7] John Francis Campion, one of the outstanding mining men of the West, came to Leadville about 1879. Many mining properties passed through his hands. He was General Manager of the Ibex Mining Company, a director of the Carbonate National Bank of Leadville, vice president of the Denver National Bank and of the Denver, Northwester and Pacific Railway.

[8] Descriptions by Mrs. Melissa Hayden and George Robinson.

off the Hill in a buggy built for two, drawn by two large white horses. Revett, in the togs of a mining engineer, weighs down the driver's side, and beside him, riding high and stiff in manifest discomfort, sits a personage in conventional black topped by a hard, black Derby hat.

Still another relic of Revett's avoirdupois is the account, highly savored by a fellow traveler, name withheld, of one of this sallies into Mexico hunting gold. Examination of a prospect was in progress, with Revett in the van, proceeding with his customary spacious tread. It so happened that a Mexican laborer quite near him, at work in the prospect hole, dropped his pick to watch the spectacle and uttered: "Holy Mother of God, when this hombre meets his death may it be near the graveyard."

TURNS TO DREDGING

There is no direct proof in any of the surviving material that Revett's attention was turning to dredging for gold in the Breckenridge District until 1894, though there is little doubt that he had it in mind, since deep digging in a Montana field had begun in 1891.[9] By that time every other method had been used in the Breckenridge District: by arastra, by panning, by rocker, by sluice and riffle, by boom, by tunneling, drifting, milling, and by Giants that washed down whole river benches.[10] But as for

---

[9] First dredge in use October 7, 1891, according to *Daily Independent*, Helena; Montana.

[10][Ed.] Turnbull's list of methods here is both diverse and exhaustive; furthermore, she progresses from "surface mining" techniques, which tend to be simpler and practicable by individual miners or propsectors, to "deep mining" techniques, which are usually not feasible without the significant technology, manpower, and capital only a corporation could bring to bear. An *arastra* (or *arrastra*) is a crude mill of ancient design—often handmade and powered by mule, horse, or human motion—which crushes the ore, thus separating the hard rock from the soft metal. *Panning*, as stated in note 1, is the most recognizable form of placer mining, and involves manually sifting and shaking gold away from sediment by use of a specially shaped pan. The *rocker*, a refinement on panning, consists of a movable hopper with a bottom of perforated metal, suspended over a contraption of canvas and wood—the machine is shaken (or rocked) while water is poured over the material collected in the hopper; sand will be shaken off the material and will settle in a tray at the bottom, while gold will be shaken off and get caught on the canvas. In the *sluice and riffle* method, the sediment-rich water passes through artificially constructed channels

(cont.)

using a dredge to bring up the precious stuff, that was considered unprofitable in a high mountain country crammed with rocks not only huge, not only packed by glaciers, but so deep in ancient channels as to resist whatever power then was in use in North America.

But Ben Stanley Revett had been cast in a different mould. He believed that this new method could be brought about. For all his smooth facade, he was a bulldog for tenacity, and unlike the bulldog he was resourceful and persuasive. And, besides all that, he knew a man who was working along the same line that he himself proposed to take. This man, wo signed his letters "S. S. Harper," was managing the Bannock gold dredge. Harper, though a cautious man, thought such a venture as Revett proposed just might bye successful, even under harder conditions than those he was working with.

Harper and Revett joined forces early in 1894, for the building and operation of deep mining.[11] Revett was chief promoter for their undertaking. Harper furnished his experience and acted wherever possible as a brake to his partner's enthusiasm. Two other partners are sometimes mentioned in Harper's letters, but by first name only. [...]

[The purchase of placer grounds] required a strong backing, and this backing was forthcoming. The list of persons ready and willing to furnish stately sums for Revett's projects would, if not destroyed, fill many pages. For in the art of promotion Revett was an adept. The backgrounds of his success in that line was

---

sluices, often made of wood); lighter sediments, such as sand, are washed away, heavier elements, such as gold, are caught on blocks of wood or stone (the riffles) which have been specially positioned within each sluice. The *boom* Turnbull mentions may refer to a mechanical system for repositioning boulders, common to hydraulic mining. *Tunneling* and *drifting* refer to the installation of tunnels to remove "wash materials" disturbed by the detonation of dynamite charges embedded in specially dug trenches (the drifts). *Milling*, like the arastra, separates metal from rock by pulverization, but uses a river wheel or even electric current to power the process—using much of the same technology common for the sawing of lumber or refinement of grain. The *Giants* were massive systems of hydraulic pumps, hoses, and jointed, rifled nozzles which allowed entire banks of debris to be broken down without the use of pick or shovel. (See *Placer Mining* and Van Bueren.)

[11]Harper letters in Revett Papers.

at least threefold: first, as is well-known in the District, Revett never promoted a sale of stock in any undertaking which was not founded on proof of excellent prospects, or in which he did not believe himself. Second, he dealt only with whom he called *strong people*. And third, his appearance of solidity and honorableness was not belied by results.

This does not mean that no criticisms were made from time to time by his associates as other traits in his character became apparent during the working out of his purposes. One of these was that his belief in whatever he was undertaking made too bright a glow, obscuring probable difficulties. A few words from an early prospectus issued undated should throw light on this trait of his:

> As this process of dredging consists merely of raising gravel from bedrock to surface and washing same into short sluices, man will thus continue the design of Nature in the simplest manner and aid to a successful completion the work of enriching the world.

"Consists merely"—what words for even the least elaborate of the processes which the early gold dredges went through in order to bring up a digger full of gravel!

And there were other traits in Revett's character that will be dealt with later in this paper, which were displeasing to his associates.

DIFFICULTIES AROSE

No dredging was done; no dredge, even begun in 1895. The whole year was taken up with examination of the ground. Difficulties arose, even in that process, that were not foreseen in any prospectus. One of them was the encounter with mammoth rocks that slowed up shafting operations. Though during that year exploration shifted to the use of an oil drill, the main objective—

to reach bedrock at the mouth of Galena Gulch, where there must be rich deposits—was not reached.[12]

COLORADO'S FIRST GOLD DREDGE

So it was not till 1896 that the first gold dredge to dig in Colorado ground was built and put into operation. It was a Risdon Company production. Its vital parts were made ready in the company's California plant, and since the Risdon company held stock in the first dredge, it must have been the very best they could do at that time. Parts for the dredge were shipped from the San Francisco plant, by wide gauge to Denver; by narrow gauge from Denver to Dickey, a way station on the Blue, whose little stone building has now been scrapped to make way for Denver's new reservoir on the Western Slope; and by ox team from Dickey to their destination on the lower Swan.

Lumber for the building of the dredge was Oregon fir[13] since no native timber was tough enough to take the terrific shaking which a dredge continually had to take. The dredge was built, and its machinery assembled in a pit dug for it close to the lower Swan. The boat was floated up at the pit filled and became a pond, fed by a ditch from the Swan, that furnished also the water for the boat's hydraulic system.

The Risdon, after the manner of gold dredges, was not built to move ahead at will; it was moored to the bottom of the pond by a spud[14] driven through the back of the boat, and it was further held in place by cables running from its sides to the dead men, great logs buried in the banks to its left and right. On the command of the dredgemaster to *step*, the spud was hoisted and the cables to the dead men loosened, and the boat floated ahead to the distance determined upon, when it was gain anchored and the digger, a huge shovel, set to work again.

---

[12]Revett Papers
[13]According to Revett Papers this was spelled "Oregon fur."
[14][Ed.] Here referring to a movable mooring pole, likely named for its similarities, not to a potato, but to a tool of the same name—a small, blunt chisel (OED).

To all concerned, from manager to dredgemaster to winchman to crew, and to all the watchers on the shore, it was a tremendous day when the machinery was set in motion and the digger dipped for the first time and came up dripping and dribbling its first load of soil and rock and dumped it on its divided paths, to save the gold or to return via the stacker to the pond.[15]

The rejoicing was short-lived. Not for nothing is the area known as a hard rock district. Its rocks are igneous and strongly fused and right down to the gold-bearing gravels they are present. All too soon it was abundantly clear that the Risdon was too light for digging to bedrock. It bucked at thirty feet and could dig no deeper. Also, in spite of the testholes, which had shown bedrock as running from 10 to 30 feet down, actually it varied at from 30 to 50 feet.

[...]

Nothing daunted by this failure, Revett induced his backer to put up the money for the financing of two new dredges furnished by the Bucyrus Company at Milwaukee, Wisconsin. It was still 1896, when these boats were set to digging. S. S. Harper's letters continually urged the sending of samples of free gold picked up from the test holes to the company's office. Whether this was done or not is not on record.

It is, however, suggested in an account set down verbatim by some unknown person, which contains a proposal that Revett send on to his backers samples of gold from a California placer to impress the company with a show of great results form the Swan diggings. That would have been not only dishonest but silly, since the gold of the Breckenridge District was entirely different from any California specimens.

[...]

In 1897, S. S. Harper transferred his holdings to Revett and withdrew. No reason for this move is in the records, and no further letters from him have been kept. One statement made by him in an early letter to Revett stands as one possible indication of a reason: *"Placers are the slowest sellers on earth."* Certainly the

---

[15]Revett Papers.

whole history of Revett's ventures into deep mining sheds light on the matter. George Robinson, once Revett's winchman, said: "He (Revett) was always hard put up to find money for running expenses." He added, Probably Revett should not have built such an expensive house as Swan's nest for his birds."

HOME LIFE AT SWAN'S NEST

It was on the first day of January, 1898, that Ben Stanley and Mary Griffin, the sister of Frank and Maurice Griffin, were married, and during that same year Revett built Swan's Nest, a handsome home for his wife, overlooking the Swan where it turned northwest for a short distance before entering the Blue River. That house is known, for it still stands, as the house of the wide doors—not the usual folding doors that were still popular in the 1880's, but single doors, each wide enough so that the dignity of its owner need not suffer by his having to pass through its doorway sidewise. The house throughout is wide to match its master, with spacious rooms. [...]

It was a costly house, the materials for which were brought from far places. [...] But for all this elegance the house fronts west to a hill that cuts off completely the view it should have of the valley of the Blue and the whole length of the Tenmile range beyond. Instead of the grandeur, it faces the long vista of rockpiles that hide even the Swan's final dash to meet the Blue. The inference is that what its owner most liked to see was one of his dredges digging gold.

From the time that Swan's nest was ready for, and during the whole of the Revetts' occupancy, they entertained largely and lavishly. Their house was noted for the eminence of its guests and the elegance and richness of its dinners. Revett himself was more than hearty eater, though not a heavy drinker. Choice wines were served in their proper sequence at their table, and Havanas that Breckenridge folk never fail to mention as having "cost a dollar each," were passed without stint.

Often after dinner there would be billiards for those gentlemen who preferred the game, or there would be music, which Revett's mellow tenor, enjoyed not only by his guests, but by patrons of the Denver Hotel bar in Breckenridge, four miles away. For Swan's Nest had a telephone, and so did the Denver Hotel bar, the din of which would stop when the proprietor, letting the receiver dangle from its place on the wall behind the bar, announced, "Gentlemen, Mr. Revett will now sing for you from Swan's Nest."[16]

[...]

THE CLEANUPS

The reason that the time between cleanups in the District was liable to vary was that the paystreaks in the channels were not continuous and the depth of bedrock also varied. In general a cleanup occurred whenever the dredgemaster decided it should be done. The dredge would dig long enough and deep enough to warrant stopping the boat for the process, which might take all of two days. Riffles on the gold-saving tables were first removed. A hose then washed the coarse gravel over the stops, leaving amalgam and black sand. This deposit was gathered in by scoops and dumped into a bucket, then fed into the hopper of a Long Tom rocker.[17] Quicksilver was then drained off, leaving the gold in a finely divided state. It was then melted in cupels, run into bricks and sent to the Denver mint.[18] The nuggets flattened against the bedrock, were kept separate and most of them were used as specimens.

[...]

There were, of course, accidents to the men, terrible ones: a head cut right off by the hopper that ground the usable rock; a man who leaned too far and fell afoul of the bucket coming up,

---

[16] All background information furnished by Summit County friends of Revett, chiefly by Melissa Hayden and George Robinson.

[17] [Ed.] A Long Tom is an advanced form of rocker which uses troughs and riffles to dredge for gold in higher volumes than what is possible with a standard rocker. (For more on the rocker or the riffle, see note 10 above.)

[18] Process described by George Robinson, and more or less the same on earlier boats.

was drowned. A man going off shift was seen by the winchman to start up the plank leading to the shore. But just then the boat bucked and neither the winchman, who operated in a sort of a hut high in the front of the boat, nor any of the men on shift saw him land. In a few minutes there was terrific jar, and the first thing the men knew a big red, three-cornered thing was floating on the pond. It was the man's liver.[19]

[...]

Then there was that second sinking of one of the company's boats, mentioned earlier in a list of drawbacks. In those early days of error and correction, the dredges, lacking the power to buck thick ice, had to lie idle in their frozen ponds through the long winters of the high mountain country. Then if a thaw set in, as happens in the District, when the chinook blows for days and even weeks at a time, there could be real trouble. This particular sinking happened on February 28, 1899, during what Summit County people call the "February thaw." The cause, as recorded in a telegram from Revett to the company's president in Boston, was the development of two leaks, which a careless watchman had not noticed, plus a hatchway which he had left open, plus more water on top of the ice than the boat could take.

At the time of this predicament Revett was on one of his numerous sallies outside the District. He sent a telegram, a copy of which has been saved, without the address of person to whom it was sent. It said: "Take out slowly outlet gate upper dredge dam—lower water to raise dredge—pumping out dredge not practical."[20]

[...]

A DAUGHTER IS BORN

In December, 1900, the Revett's only child was born, a daughter christened Frances. It was Frances who provided Summit County residents with significant anecdotes. According to Mrs. Hayden, during the summers of their occupation of Swan's Nest,

---

[19]Ed Auge, chronicler of the District's mining history. [Ed: This moment is fictionalized in a climactic scene from *Goldboat*, in a section published in this volume as "[Olsen]" (UM 53).]

[20]Telegram copy in Revett papers.

the Revetts entertained a noted geologist whose name she did not recall. This gentleman and the young Frances, then between four and five years of age, became great pals. One morning young Frances proposed that they two should visit a spring a little way uphill behind the house. Hand in hand the two friends made the short climb, but as they reached the spring they discovered that neither had brought a cup. Frances offered to get one, but the geologist suggested that they kneel and scoop up the water in their hands. They did, and found the water icy cold. Frances made a face. Frowning, she said, "Did you get any?"

"Not much," the man said. "Did you?"

She said, "Not one damn drop!"

That night at dinner (dinners at Swan's Nest, following the custom of English gentlepeople, did not include the young fry) the geologist told with gusto the incident at the spring. Revett roared his enjoyment, but his wife just gasped. "Now Stanley," she said, "you see what happens when you try to bring up a child properly in this rough country!"

Mrs. Hayden's comment was that the incident seemed to her indicative of the trend the Revetts' family life was taking in the Breckenridge District, where Mary Revett never came to feel at home.

[...]

THE RELIANCE COMPANY IS FORMED

Early in 1908, Revett's associates in the French Gulch operation [a recent expansion of Revett's business interests] prevailed over his continued objection to the formation of an incorporated company and the association became the Reliance Company, with Revett as its trustee. [...]

By 1910, serious trouble between Revett, as trustee of the Reliance Company, and his associates had occurred over the use of the company funds. It had become increasingly clear that

Revett was not cut out for the administration of large sums of money. More than one true friend of his has stated that he was an honorable fellow, but was not a financier; that he did not understand money; that when he saw what he considered to be a primary need to spend the company sums in a different way from what had been laid down for a specific purpose by his directors he did not consider himself accountable to them for the way it should be used. Indeed, he was known to borrow on his own hook for such a purpose, and was sometimes unable to meet his obligations when the time came for repayment. He is said by men who worked with him in the District, as well as by others who were his friends, to have won and lost three fortunes.[21]

A SUIT IN EQUITY

Lawsuits had been threatened against him and had been dropped, but in August, 1910, a suit in equity actually was filed against him. [Two English investors in Revett's French Gulch operation, C. W. Franklin and Allen G. Fairbairn, claimed Revett had withheld from them the return on their investment, even though the operation had been productive enough to pay for numerous expansions and improvements, as well as Revett's $10,000 a year salary.][22]

The suit, begun in 1909, dragged on until October, 1912, when it was settled as follows: public sale to be made of the Reliance grounds and properties; creditors first to be satisfied; Revett then to have the remainder as salary of trustee. [...] But, since only one bid was made at the required public sale, and that bid was so low as to be completely unsatisfactory, no sale was made.

Meanwhile the dredging in French Gulch went on, uninterrupted by the law's delays. [...]

On September 7, 1913, a copy of a night letter, in Revett's hand, to the President of the Colorado Consolidated Mining

[21]Trevor Thomas, ["The Revett Story," *Summit County Journal*, May 29, 1953].
[22]See also: *Denver Republican*, Feb. 19, 1911.

Company Incorporated in Lawrence, Michigan (under whose placer laws most of Revett's undertakings were incorporated) announced an offer for sale under court decree of the Reliance property and dredge. The sale was held in the same year with the one unsatisfactory low. The night letter continues: *An interested party has offered a more* satisfactory purchase Have people now ready to purchase all outstanding stock and indebtedness and built large modern dredges."

Another notation states that in 1913, stockholders of the Reliance Company were paid its principal plus interest 3%. The company's indebtedness was paid and the master in chancery appointed by the court dismissed. [...]

Another event of 1913, not mentioned, however, in the Revett papers, was the final departure of Mrs. Revett and Frances from Swan's Nest. A friend of the family in speaking of this move said that the decision was only partly due to a heart strain which Frances was said to have developed. Mrs. Revett died in San Francisco, in 1952. In that year, Frances, who had married a lawyer, was living at Crystal Bay, Nevada, where she had a studio.[23]

REVETT'S LAST DREDGING IN BRECKENRIDGE DISTRICT

The last gold dredging operation with which Revett is known in Breckenridge to have been associated was the Tonopah Placers Company, which began dredging in 1915 with three boats at work, and ran for fifteen years. Of this company Revett was consulting engineer. [...]

During the rest of his life Revett spent a good part of his time, when not traveling about to inspect deep mining projects and operations, at the Bohemian Club of San Francisco or at the Denver Club, both of which he was a member. If it is true, as has often been said, that his third fortune and his last had by then been lost, still toward the end of his life he was backed by his strong friends of many years, who saw to it that he wanted for nothing, and that he lived in high style at his clubs and in the

[23]Trevor Thomas, "The Revett Story," *Summit County Journal*, May 29, 1953.

best hotels until he died in 1937. It is said that in his last days, though plagued by illness, he was promoting the organization of a company to work over the long expanses of rock piles in the District in search of the gold that had gone out over the stackers of the dredges that had dug there.

With Ben Stanley Revett's exit from the field of gold dredging, a certain verve and polish vanished with him. True, the work went on; the last dredge to dig in the District was the Blue River boat, that dug south along the Blue till the price of labor and materials made it unprofitable to continue. The country's need for baser metals stripped the remaining hulks right down to the water line, till now nothing is left in the ponds but rotting timbers, and beyond them the long and barren mounds of tailings that fill the valley bottoms and the gulches, all but obliterating even a glimpse here and there of great stretches of the Swan, the French, and the Blue.

Belle Turnbull in her senior frock (1903).

POVERTY GULCH AND MENDICANT RIDGE: PROSPECTING FOR THE REAL COLORADO

George Sibley

GEORGE SIBLEY is a freelance writer and retired faculty from Western State Colorado University, where he taught journalism and regional studies. He has coordinated such projects as the annual Headwaters Conference, Water Workshop, and Environmental Symposium. His most recent work is Water Wranglers, *a commissioned history of the Colorado River District and the development of Colorado's share of the Colorado River, published by the Colorado River District. His essays and articles have appeared in* Harper's, High Country News, New Age Journal, Old West, *and many more.*

———◆———

Mountains cast spells on me—
 Why, because of the way
Earth-heaps lie, should I be
Choked by joy mysteriously;
 Stilled or drunken-gay?

—*Belle Turnbull, "Mountain-Mad"*

The truth is, a place is more than half memory. No place is a place until things that have happened in it are remembered in history, ballads, yarns, legends, or monuments…. No place, not even a wild place, is a place until it has had that human attention that at its highest reach we call poetry.

—*Wallace Stegner*

This is not directly an essay about Belle Turnbull; it is an attempt to recreate the context in which Belle Turnbull lived and wrote poetry, an attempt to create a sense of her Colorado. I write it not from a perspective of academic objectivity, but as one who has done time in roughly the same Colorado—and as one who oscillates between feeling uncomfortable and rejoicing in the presence of her best poetic creation, the prospector Mr. Probus.

"Sense of place" is a phrase that gets used and abused often today, with the usual loss of what it might actually mean. Try to pin it down and it gets as slippery as a fish. But as a Coloradan, I also find "Colorado" to be a slippery word: is Colorado a place? About which one can or should have a "sense" if one is truly a Coloradan? And if so, who are the poets who have made it a place?

I'll jump into it bluntly: no, Colorado as we see it on the map is not a place. We Americans are a nation-state of states that mostly make no sense geographically or ecologically. Many of our states are defined by one or two boundaries that are sensible, following some natural division or feature in the landscape—a river, a mountain ridge, a transitional zone. But almost invariably they are defined by other boundaries that are simply straight lines imposed blindly over whatever geography is actually there down on the ground, lines that ignore all natural phenomena, and usually end up complicating subsequent political, economic and cultural life.

This process of defining states by straight lines approached the absurd in the American West, and nowhere more so than in Colorado, an abstraction that was carved out of the Kansas and Nevada Territories, which had at least used the Continental Divide as their mutual border. But that bit of good sense was lost in 1860 when the early unsettlers defined themselves by four longitudinal and latitudinal lines whose only rationale seemed to be to make sure they were highgrading all of the mineral wealth of the Southern Rocky Mountains.

The resulting State of Colorado is a simplistic rectangle imposed over some of the most diverse and complex geography on the planet. I think of the mapped state as a blanket draped over a fence, covering more than it shows. Within those lines, meaningful only to ships at sea using celestial navigation, are at least five very distinct regions, each with its own natural ecology and human culture. The Colorado Humanities Council some time ago described "Five Colorados" as distinct cultural entities ("Five States"). I'm thinking along similar lines but with distinct variations.

The eastern third of the rectangle is the High Plains, a drier continuation of the Great Plains that stretch all the way from the Mississippi River—big-farm country with a residual agrarian culture that's being overrun by agribusiness. Culturally, that part of Colorado is more bonded to the Midwestern states.

On the other side of the state—the westernmost part of the rectangle, including the San Juan Basin on the southern edge—is the high orographic desert of the Colorado Plateau: a canyon-cut steppe-desert where Indian and Mormon cultures coexist, aided in that by the large spaces and deep canyons among them.

The southeastern quadrant of the state, the upper Rio Grande Basin and the southern tributaries of the Arkansas River, is high dry plains—the *llanos*—dropping into the drier and hotter subtropical deserts: a region whose cultural compass has historically pointed toward Old and New Mexico much longer than there has been a Colorado or United States.

Those three subregions of the abstract Colorado are all culturally bonded to the larger ecologies and economies from which they were artificially sliced by the abstract Colorado boundaries; they are only bound to "Colorado" by state governance—and also through highly ambiguous relationships with a fourth Colorado: the metropolitan cluster of growing cities and suburbs along the piedmont region generally called Denver, a city related to both mountains and plains in the same way a port city is related to the ocean.

Four out of every five people who call themselves Coloradans live in that growing metro complex, with which the other one-in-five of us have a serious love-hate relationship: we enjoy the Broncos and Rockies the cities support, and we have to appreciate, however reluctantly, the churn of business that produces virtually everything we need to live in the rest of the state—a dependency that embarrasses and alarms us: when a blizzard shuts down the city for a few days, our grocery shelves go empty even though the storm might miss us entirely. We are also grimly aware of our dependence on the city (all the great global cities, for that matter) as a market for virtually everything we produce, including good places to vacation—and we are also grimly aware of the city's voracious needs, especially for water.

Those four parts of the Colorado rectangle might be "places" by Stegner's standards—but those places are not "Colorado." Willa Cather and Kent Haruf speak for that part of the Midwest east of the cities; Rudolph Anaya and Aaron Abeyta speak for the people of the southeastern *llanos*; N. Scott Momaday and Ed Abbey speak for the spectrum of the Colorado Plateau. Denver Colorado has had a number of journalist-poets like Thomas Hornsby Ferril and Ed Quillen who ventured to pull it all together around the city region as the Rocky Mountain Empire, but it is increasingly an indistinguishable terminal of a global city made up of the same corporations, chains, and franchises whose poets are often as abstract and placeless as its economy.

But there's yet another part of that rectangle—the mountain part of the state, a Colorado defined by elevation, Colorado above 6,000-6,500 feet elevation. This is where Colorado began as a state of mind before it became misidentified with an overreaching abstraction on a map. And Belle Turnbull may be the most important of the poets doing the "remembering" that has turned that state of mind into a place by Stegner's standards.

But what was, or is, the state of mind that took root in the mountains (and in Belle Turnbull), that became the true Colorado? That is what we are assaying here.

Intolerable the marching of this range,
This fugue of sight unbroken and immense,
In theme and counterpoint forever strange,
Forever overflowing human sense.
Impose upon your lips the native game
Of undertruth, the minimum of awe:
At sunset when the snowsmoke drifts in flame
Say it is pretty, presently withdraw [...]
("Window on the Range," TMR 35; UM: 85)

A place to begin in looking at this "real Colorado" is to understand the name itself, "*colorado*." It's a Spanish adjective—not a noun, which makes it a little odd for the name of a place. But it is also generally mistranslated. Ask any Coloradan today how it translates to English, and they will probably say "red"; *Colorado* means "red." But isn't *rojo* "red"? Yes—but so what, so is *colorado*, everyone says so.

But dig into "*colorado*" a little, with a personal spoon rather than the steam shovel of convention, and you find a much more linguistically obvious and expansive meaning. In an internet discussion on the topic of the meaning of *colorado*, one person drew on the authority of the Spanish Royal Academy Dictionary to declare that "red or reddish is just a secondary meaning of '*colorado*'" (Rodriguez). As the word's root itself suggests—indeed seems to shout—*colorado* means, primarily, "having color," any color. "Colorful Colorado," as the billboards say: Colorado *colorado*.

So what, then, is the color of our mountain Colorado? One can find a lot of red, if one looks for it, but that was not the color the first Coloradans were looking for in 1859, when Colorado was still just a state of mind for the prospectors swarming up every stream and gulch tributary to the upper South Platte River—and even over the Great Divide into the Blue River valley, headwaters for the Colorado River, all within a matter of months that first year: Belle Turnbull's beloved Breckenridge, at 9,600 feet elevation on the West Slope, applied for and got its post office the same year—1859—as the merely mile-high Denver area mining camps.

And what was the color of this Colorado in 1859? The color they were seeing in their flat pans (or tin cups) when they shouted out, "She's showin' color!" Gold first, and then silver too, were the original colors infusing the state of mind that drove otherwise intelligent men and women to leave their old lives behind and swarm up the wild rivers and streams of this Colorado.

We know that even then Colorado *colorado* had other even more vivid colors—the reds, blues, and shadows of the mountains often capped in white, the vast textured slopes of dark green conifer forest and light green aspen forest, the high meadows with their paisley carpets of flowers, the lower gray-green meadows dropping down to soft green floodplains, laced by the meandering rivers seasonally running from muddy red to clear greenish, fed by the myriad tumbling whitewater creeks.

But in the beginning, in that first basement epoch of Colorado as a state of mind, Colorado's other colors were not just ignored, they were in the way. Whole green hillsides were washed down in hydraulic mining; dark green forests that weren't cut down fast enough for boomtown lumber were burned to expose rock outcrops; dredges literally plowed rich green floodplains into intestinal coils of sterile gray rubble. Streams and rivers occasionally still change to very strange colors with runoff from abandoned mines. Colorado's first colors, the gold and silver, all disappeared into Denver banks and mansions; much of the gray-brown mess that this pillage engendered lingers on here into the present.

But the prospectors and miners—and farmers who came along to feed mining towns that were living out of tin cans—left another legacy, less destructive and more interesting: the names that might be first stage in creating a place. Most of the names on our map of headwaters Colorado come from that early era—several categories of names.

Least interesting are the mundane, obvious names—all those Brush Creeks, Clear Creeks, Muddy Creeks, and Bald Mountains. Also the places just named unimaginatively for the first Anglo unsettler in the place—the town of Irwin, the Smith Fork, Taylor Park.

There are the obligatory honorific names like Gunnison River, named for Captain John Gunnison who led the first official expedition along it; there are all the Mt. Garfields and Mt. Emmons named for presidents and governors. (A little mendacity went into some of these names; the Denver camp—still part of the Kansas Territory—was named for the governor of Kansas, and Breckenridge was named for the vice-president of the United States, in hope of expediting the post office application.)

We have mountains and other natural features named for native peoples otherwise generally badly treated: Ouray Peak, Chipeta Falls, Ute Mountain, Curecanti Creek.

There is a whole category of what I think of as the homesick names, mostly named by the farmers that followed the prospectors: Ohio Creek, Virginia Peak, Missouri Flats.

Higher up, a lot of the names are drawn from the miners' own experiences in pursuit of their dreams of gold and silver: Mineral Point, Ruby Range, Treasury Peak, Silver Creek, Quartz Creek. Oh-be-joyful Creek near Crested Butte is a less obvious member of this name-group, but it is probably evocative of the feeling that swept over many a prospector as he panned into a patch of gravel showing color.

But there is something a little biblical about most of those names: humans charged by God, under Manifest Destiny, to go name everything, and thereby have dominion over it all. Naming a new place after a place one has left seems a likely way to miss seeing what is new in the new place, as does naming it narrowly in terms of its yield of material wealth. There is no real "sense of place" in that—at least not in the sense defined by western poet David Wagoner: "You must treat [the place] as a powerful stranger, / Must ask permission to know it and be known" ("Lost").

There are some other categories of names, however, that are more reflective in one way or another—names that bespeak some degree of sensitivity to being in the presence of powerful strangers, or at least a powerful strangeness. These are poetic names, mythic names, sometimes serious, sometimes more serious.

Some of those who came here stood still long enough to hear and adopt the names given to places here by people who had preceded them here for centuries. Names like Curecanti, Cochetopa, Tomichi. Western Slope poet Mark Todd wrote about "Tomichi Creek," where he lives:

> Tumit Che: words in Ute
> that mean "mountain stream."
> It's the headwater-trickle
> through tundra, a cascade,
> a passage that wears rock
> with time and flow.
>
> ("Tumit Che:")

That is the poet coming to Here and stopping, looking and listening—a key to getting permission to know a place, and to help make it a place.

But that earliest period of this particular Colorado *colorado* as a state of mind—I think of it as the Fool's Gold period—was marked by yet another trace of name-giving that struck me as slim and erratic evidence that some of those prospectors who came here had enough of the soul of the poet to see beyond, and even laugh about, their own mundane folly in looking for the Fool's Gold. Belle Turnbull's alter ego, Mr. Probus, is the touchstone for this breed of prospector:

> Yet I that had my dreamings otherwise,
> That fought the rock and lost, and always lost,
> Have on this hill my freehold and my skies [...]
>
> ("Miner's Pension," TMR 25; UM 81)

There were literary and aesthetic references in the naming of places—a dumpy muddy little mining town named Ophir, after a fabulous biblical port city ("Ophir" means "gold" in Hebrew); another town named Ilium, the Roman name for Troy. The City of Montrose was named for a 17th century Scottish Royalist immortalized by Sir Walter Scott (no wonder they are mostly Republicans). Gothic Mountain near Crested Butte was so named for the pattern of pointed arches eroded on its face.

Such names suggest people educated enough to know their own history—perhaps even to know when they were repeating it. That is embodied in Turnbull's Mr. Probus, with his wry, self-aware and self-deprecating wit—a composite of the old prospectors still hanging out in her mountain town a quarter-century after the boom, "so long / As [they] can claw a tunnel, with the strong / Smell of the ore beyond […] and raise the song / Of victory too soon" ("Hardrock Miner," TMR 22; UM 78).

But Turnbull's wryly philosophical Mr. Probus leads me on to another, even fainter and thinner vein of color in this literary-aesthetic naming in our mountain Colorado—call it the "Poverty Gulch" phenomenon. Poverty Gulch is a relatively rich silver-mining watershed up the Slate River from Crested Butte, in the Gunnison River basin. In that same vein, I was once part-owner of an 1890 patented mining claim upvalley in the Gunnison Basin named on the deed the "No Hope No. 3." And another: for a number of years, up in the Smith Fork valley near Crawford, out the window by my desk, I could see a long spur of highland called Mendicant Ridge.

The No Hope No. 3 was apparently accurately named—and probably preceded by the No Hope Nos. 1 & 2. But Poverty Gulch had the Augusta Mine, a pretty rich mine, relatively speaking—so why Poverty Gulch? What was the state of mind behind those sort of depressed names, found here and there throughout the mining districts? I can think of a couple possible explanations. Easiest explanation: put on the poor face, and you won't have such a crowded neighborhood.

But a second explanation—and this is tenuous—is a kind of self-conscious irony. Many of the individuals who came to the Rockies on the pretext of looking for gold, something most of them knew absolutely nothing about, were probably borderline crazy—or at least considered themselves to be so, in the contexts of an urbanizing industrializing society that made them feel a little crazy. Like Melville's Ishmael, trying to restrain himself from "stepping into the street and methodically knocking people's hats off"; under such self-imposed pressures, some headed for the ocean, some for the desert, others for the mountains. Most of them were post-urbanites terminally tired of becoming ever more industrially organized; some of them were well educated in a society that only valued "business smarts"; some, maybe many of them later in the 1860s, were probably Civil War PTSD survivors self-aware enough to know they'd best head for places as wild as they were. And—like their counterparts still arriving in this Colorado today—some of them were self-reflective enough to know that what they were doing was borderline crazy.

So for this stony mudhole where you're laboring under the ridiculous hope that it will somehow make you fabulously wealthy—if you aren't going to name it after Troy or Ophir with a chuckle, what better name than Poverty Gulch (with the same chuckle)?

"I have to laugh," Mr. Probus says, "I have to laugh" ("Time as a Well-Spring," TMR 19; UM 75). And in that ironic laugh Probus—and his creator—embrace both the easy illusions that lead us to the mountains and the harder realities we find there, where we can be simultaneously "choked by joy mysteriously" and driven indoors by the "intolerable marching of this range ... forever overflowing human sense":

> Never along that range is ease:
> Things are warped that are too near heaven,
> Ink runs clotted down the pen,
> Verse has the twist of timberline trees.
>
> ("Foreword," TMR 11; UM 70)

Other people have written about living in the Colorado mountains, and continue to do so today—I'm guilty of it myself. Much of it is beautiful work—earnest and heartfelt celebrations of the beauty and grandeur of the place. Much of what is written about these places also has a macho "men to match my mountains" strain, especially when the mining era is the focus. The magnificence, the beauty, the challenge of it all seems to be the driver of this prose and poetry.

But I have encountered no other Colorado writer who so authentically captures the ambiguity of life in these high places as Turnbull does—the ironic self-awareness that enables one to behold the ambiguity implicit in the magnificence and meanness of the mountains without feeling the usual American need to match, conquer, extract, or otherwise eliminate ambiguity. A century earlier, John Keats wrote about "Negative Capability [...] when man is capable of being in uncertainties, mysteries, doubts, without any irritable reaching after fact & reason" (277)— capable, perhaps, of simply being in the moment, letting the poetry take the poet where it wants, the way mountain weather does. Nobody does that better than Belle Turnbull—especially in her nine-sonnet cycle exploring Mr. Probus and his world. Irony, Turnbull believed, was the "sterner relative" of humor—a way of looking sidelong, askance but empathetic, at something in oneself deeper, more serious. So despite Mr. Probus's constant poking fun at himself for his "dreamings ... that fought the rock and lost, and always lost," it never seemed to be just about mining:

> I have my castle, Probus said, and when
> I shall have done with this godawful hole,
> Broken my pick and shinnied up the pole,
> I shall go forth and view its spires again.
> ("Lunch Time in the Tunnel," TMR 20; UM 76)

Probus becomes the first and still one of the most artfully rendered literary characters to capture the full range of human life in the Colorado ranges: his ambition always mixed with resignation, his hope comfortable with the probability of failure, his love of the mountains overlaid with frustration at what the mountains withheld—but always, with all of that, "I have to laugh, he said, I have to laugh."

Back to Poverty Gulch for a moment—and Mendicant Ridge. Colorado rhymes with Eldorado, the fabulous city of gold that was supposed to be even richer than the already-plundered cities of Mexico and Peru; and Colorado is somewhere in the region vaguely north of Mexico where were supposed to exist the equally fabulous Seven Cities of Cibola. The Euro-American unsettlers came seeking them—first the Spanish-Americans coming north with cross and sword seeking pillage for god and king, then the Anglo-Americans coming west with pick and shovel assuming Eldorado to be a do-it-yourself project. A few fortunes were taken out of the mountains, mostly invested in the "great and growing cities" that could maybe pass for the fabulous Seven Cities if you don't look too closely.

But no one would have mistaken Breckenridge for a city of gold in the 1930s, when Turnbull and her life partner Helen Rich (also a writer) moved there. And Turnbull never gilded the lily in her perceptions of the Breckenridge she knew. (Although she did live long enough to see the beginning of its ski-resort era; was that what Mr. Probus called "newer outfits sweating hope and blood" raising in place of the old "goldleaf" god "yet more preposterous gods?" ["Opus 8," TMR 26; UM 82])

Her only prose novel, *The Far Side of the Hill*, was set in a small Colorado mountain town (name changed to "Topas" to protect the guilty) that was—by another Stegner standard—certainly not a society to match its scenery. The same could have been said— probably still could be—for the towns I "found" in the Upper Gunnison River valley in the 1960s. Despite the current glitter of resort hotels and big second homes, these are places that are still hard places to actually live and work in for us Probuses; by all our sophisticated economic measures, they are all some variant on "Poverty Gulch."

Yet people like Belle Turnbull and Helen Rich continue to come into this mountain Colorado, everyone prospecting for something or other even if they aren't exactly sure what for, or even really conscious of it. "Prospect" is another slippery word: it can be a verb and a noun—even (like *colorado*) an adjective, as in all the "sense-of-place" real estate developments named "Prospect Park." As a noun, it can refer to something as narrow and small as a potentially good vein of quartz in a granite wall, or to something as expansive as a grand vista where one seems able to see all the way to the future. The latter being easier to find than the former, although not always easy to get to. Mendicant Ridge is a good hike above Poverty Gulch.

But there I have to make a distinction that I think contains a difference. A mendicant (oh these slippery words) is one who deliberately seeks material poverty to see what is on the far side of it. Consider Belle Turnbull—living on "the far side of the hill" in post-mining, pre-skiing Breckenridge, the epitome of "Poverty Gulch": was Turnbull a mendicant? Am I, having lived above 7,000 feet for most of the past half-century without a lot to show for it, a mendicant? Are the new university grads here, applying their degrees waiting tables and shoveling snow because they're "just not ready to leave yet," mendicants?

Well, yes and no. We're all prospectors, like Turnbull and her Mr. Probus, and the prospect is always there, as Mr. Probus observes:

> Soon as a bluebird settles on a fence,
> Two shall string out and beat it up the trail,
> A jackass first, a miner at his tail.
>
> ("Hardrock Miner," TMR 22; UM 78)

So that is Belle Turnbull's Colorado, the true and only Colorado; one day we're in Poverty Gulch, the next day maybe pushing our ass up Mendicant Ridge—where maybe we will be given permission to stumble onto the true gold, the philosopher's stone, in the bolt of a moment—like Turnbull:

How am I to tell you?
I saw a bluebird
a bluebird incandescent
flying up the pass

and where the wind came over
the Great Divide came over
invisible and mighty
he struck a wall of glass.

I saw his bright wings churning
I saw him stand in heaven
the bird's power   the wind's power
miraculously hold—

Now I will tell you
dare my soul to say it
speak the name of beauty
accurate and cold.

("Observations Above Timberline," T 2; UM 93)

I have to laugh, sometimes, myself—incredulous at being blessed to see such things, such sudden and powerful beauty in places so majestically demanding and often unforgiving or just not giving, and I thank Belle Turnbull for helping us to see this, so accurate and cold. I have to laugh.

WORKS CITED

"Five States of Colorado, The." *Colorado Humanities*, The Colorado Humanities Counil, http://www.coloradohumanities.org/content/five-states-colorado-•-intro

Keats, John. "To George and Thomas Keats." 22 Dec. 1817. *The Complete Poetical Works and Letters of John Keats*. Edited by Horace Elisha Scudder, Cambridge Edition, Riverside, 1899: pp. 276-77.

Rodriguez, Felipe. Comment on "A bit of Colorado Color." *Digital Photography Review*, 3 Nov. 2011, www.dpreview.com/forums/post/39753422

Todd, Mark. "Tumit Che:" *Wire Song*, Conundrum, 2001: p. 41.

Wagoner, David. "Lost." *Poetry*, vol. 118, no. 4, Jul. 1971: p. 219.

A WAY OF SEEING: BELLE TURNBULL'S GEOGRAPHY OF LOVE

Susan Spear

SUSAN SPEAR, poet and librettist, holds an MFA in poetry with an emphasis in versecraft from Western State Colorado University. She teaches poetry and creative writing at Colorado Christian University in Lakewood, Colorado. Her poems have appeared in Academic Questions, The Anglican Theological Review, Mezzo Cammin, Measure, *and other journals. Her manuscript* In Ordinary Time *was a semi-finalist for the Crab Orchard First Book Prize. She serves as the Managing Editor of* THINK, *a journal of poetry, reviews, and criticism housed at Western State.*

A lover's eye sees and memorizes the appearance of the beloved in totality and in minute detail: the entirety of the beloved's appearance from across a room or meadow, but also small signature features such as beauty marks or uniquely colored irises. A lover appreciates even the tiny imperfections of the beloved; all features are equally endearing. Such is love, and this way of seeing is not limited to the love between two human beings. On occasion, an author falls so deeply in love with a landscape that it becomes a character. Think of Faulkner's Yoknapatawpha County, Steinbeck's Monterey, Jeffers' Big Sur, Frost's New Hampshire, and Kathleen Norris' Dakota. The American West still inspires this kind of romance. One of its lovers was, surprisingly, Nabokov. As Landon Y. Jones recently put it, "Something about the Rocky Mountain West reminded Nabokov of his youth in Russia. 'Some part of me must have been born in Colorado,' he wrote to the critic Edmund Wilson, 'for I am constantly recognizing things with a delicious pang.'"

It is with that lover's "delicious pang" that Belle Turnbull, born in New York but raised in Colorado Springs, writes of Summit County, Colorado, and its backdrop of the Tenmile Range. She bases her fictional mountain towns of Topas and Rockinghorse on Breckenridge. In both prose and verse, Turnbull precisely and compellingly captures the grand landscape, the minutiae of the terrain, the creatures of the Rockies, and the miners and other sturdy folk who choose to live there year-round. No one did it as well before her, and few have since. She was an original.

The Far Side of the Hill and *Goldboat*, Turnbull's two novels in prose and verse respectively, both begin with a long shot description of what a traveler would see driving over the Great Divide into her imagined towns. In *The Far Side of the Hill*, as the Jessers return from a suffocating trip to a funeral on the Western Slope, Turnbull describes two views of Topas:

> Under that hump, [outsiders] say, is Topas village […] It lies in what is called up there a basin, and if you don't mind a stretch of shelf road and some pretty stiff grades and three or four hairpin turns where you are likely to meet yourself coming back around, why, it might be worth your while to find out how pretty it can be at the top end of a Divide County road […]
>
> And yet to a dozen families or so Topas is at the core of life. It is the flat country below that to them is a long way off and hard to come at. Topas people refer to open country as Outside, and they go to such places grudgingly and come back from them with all possible speed. (FSH 1-2)

And thus she begins a story that carries the theme of life Inside and life Outside through the novel. It is a theme that ultimately determines how the story resolves. A love of the Rockies, particularly the land above timberline, decides the trajectory of life for those characters who are Inside.

Goldboat opens similarly. Again, Turnbull describes the view a driver sees when crossing the Continental Divide. In this multi-sensory description, she presents both the long view and the tight perspective:

> Or a man may twist his wheel where a wild road
>   feathers
> Under a range that marches on a valley,
> Turn and be gone away to Rockinghorse country,
> Wind through a park beside its swaggering river,
> Creep on a shelf around a rocky shoulder,
> Check in a pasture, by a waterpit
> Under a rocksnake of cold blue cobbles mounded.
>
> Still pond, no moving. And a wooden bird,
> A squat hightailing monstrous waterwidgeon
> Diving its chain of spoonbills down and under
> Red-rusted in the turquoise pit.
> No moving. And no sound from the grotesque
> Impossible of vision.
>
> (GB 1; UM 42)

It is Turnbull's fond eye that sees and reports the "chain of spoonbills," the "turquoise" color, and the striking absence of movement and sound that becomes the backdrop for her novel of mining and romance. This harsh setting, gorgeous but often dangerous, plays the role of a character in the novel.

Turnbull's Rocky Mountains are not snow-capped blue mountain peaks surveyed from a safe distance. The men work the mines, women fish for sustenance as well as sport, they all keep their homes, fall in love, gossip, confide in one another, and survive together among the elements. In this landscape, however, unlike the many fanciful or sentimental writers of the region before and since, Turnbull takes careful notice of the small and singular. In "This Fir," an otherwise uncollected poem included by Robert McCracken and Karen Fisher in *Voice of the Mountains*, she ponders a fir tree. Not fir trees, plural, but "this fir-tree," a solitary tree in relation to a human being. She both admires the fir and questions its existence:

> Is a fir noble? is a fir
> jade-springing? *Is* a fir?
> Wind, hail upon it, sun
> upon it: to know sun upon
> this fir-tree, in the looping brain
> what flashes, what vibrations running
> cell to cell, and beauty born
> that moment out of a glue of matter
> on rod and cone hung upside down! Then
> when rod and cone and brain are gone
> and the last poem blown nowhere
> is a fir not, with none to care?
>
> (McCracken and Fisher 9; UM 112)

She asks the old, but never tired, question concerning the relationship of nature and human beings. Will the fir exist if there is no poet or person to know it? The poem's syntax, its long ecstatic fragment in the moment of knowing the fir, answers the question in the poem itself, for we now continue to ponder "this fir-tree" through this poem.

This picture of a fir is a close shot of life along the Tenmile Range, but Turnbull zooms in even more closely in "Brother Juniper," another uncollected poem published in the *Washington Post* in 1942. The title indicates her kinship to this common mountain tree, and the lines offer careful attention to the details of her beloved landscape:

> Under the primrose cliffs
> Lives an old juniper,
> Claws like a hippogriff's
> Fastened round a rock.

> Warworn his trunk is,
> Rigid his fiber,
> Ribboned his bark.
>   For all his payment,
> Wrung as a tear is,
> Pale on his raiment
> Of ashen green:
> Four frosty berries,
> Issue of the ages,
> Juiceless and lean.
>
> (McCracken and Fisher 12)

Those familiar with the juniper know that the trees are usually replete with dark-colored, "frosty" berries. In this poem, Turnbull speaks of a lone tree with a meager four "juiceless" and "lean" berries. Nothing is too sparse or too beleaguered for her attention.

Turnbull does not stop singing of small things with the juniper berry. She must have been partial to the pasque flower, for she versifies it in at least two poems. The word "pasque" is French for Easter; the small lilac and yellow colored flowers are thus named because they bloom during the Easter season and are harbingers of spring. Turnbull celebrates the cycle of the seasons in "Pasque Flowers." This poem of three beat lines and exquisite rhyme (amethyst / unearthliest) is tiny like the flower it honors:

> The earth's in cataclysm,
> storm-bound, deprived of Heaven:
> Yet round the wasteland these
> punctual presences
> stand up in amethyst,
> mist-whorled, unearthliest:
> Deep-footed against death
> Springs the returning wreath.
>
> (T 6; UM 97)

Turnbull more explicitly sings of the ineffable hope that accompanies spring after a long, struggle with the death and hardship of winter in the mountains in a similar poem, "Colorado Easter." She is astonished at this small, blooming expression: "… Flushed, lilac, washen blue—/ God, did You ever do / A lovelier deed than dress / Pasque-flowers in hopefulness?" (McCracken and Fisher 8; first appeared in *The Lyric West* in April, 1924). Again, in a short three-beat line Turnbull expresses wonder over this delicate bloom of hope.

In the same way that she notices tiny berries and blossoms, Turnbull pays attention to birds. "Observations Above Timberline" speaks of the brilliant, incandescence of a bluebird. The poem recounts the poet seeing:

> a bluebird incandescent
> flying up the pass
>
> […]
>
> I saw his bright wings churning
> I saw him stand in heaven
> the bird's power   the wind's power
> miraculously hold—
>
> Now I will tell you
> dare my soul to say it
> speak the name of beauty,
> accurate and cold.

(т 2; um 93)

The poet sees both the sweeping power of the wind and the powerful beauty of the tiny bluebird holding its place in space. She captures the Tenmile Range in both the great and the small.

In the "Probus" poems, her prize-winning sonnet sequence in the persona of the seasoned mountain man and miner Mr. Probus, the blue jay has a similar function, though ironic in this case. In "Miner's Pension," Probus speaks of his "dalliance with heaven on a hill" and the "angels" who "swarm past Probus-sill / Setting their feathers in a gentle steam / To flutter queries that a jay might deem / Too rowdy for his modesty to spill" (TMR 25; um 81). Through the voice of Probus, Turnbull pokes gentle fun at the loud birds which a noisy jay might "deem / Too rowdy." Could Turnbull be figuratively alluding to the loneliness of the tough miner and the superficial "dalliances" that do not provide the satisfaction of a loving relationship? Yet, the title indicates that the setting is ample pension for the man. *Goldboat* mentions the sound of the thrush: "...All she could hear / Was the matter-of-fact of a willow thrush proclaiming / Last of the summer birds his simple views" (GB 26). This poet's birds are carefully observed creatures, seen from various points of view, both literal and metaphorical.

In addition to the bluebird, jay, and thrush, Turnbull's addresses less benign beasts. The ballad "In Those Rude Airs" tells a bone-chilling story. The second stanza ends with the refrain, "Wolverines move ruthless there, / Wildcats too, but men the most" (TMR 44; um 87) which repeats as the last two lines of the poem. In this story, Turnbull shows that even in the pristine beauty of Summit County all is not always well. "Ruthless" wolves and wildcats prowl, but men are "the most" ruthless. The ballad tells of Whitey and Red, two laconic trappers. Red manages to "snare" a wife, and folks predict there may be trouble between Red's bride and Whitey. One morning in spring, Whitey appears at the door of Sagehen, the wise old woman who serves as both midwife and mortician. She leaves with him, and in the evening she returns with two people behind her pulling a loaded sled. The sled leaves, and a friend comes to Sagehen's cabin. After three "hot ones," Sagehen speaks without restraint:

> He said she'd a yen for rabbit stew,
> Tripped on a root and blew her brains.
>
> Twenty below at dawn, if one;
> Her blood had froze her to that door
> She laid on...Now I ask of you,
> What did she hunt in slippers for?

(TMR 46; um 89)

Red's wife did not accidentally shoot herself while hunting. In this poem, Turnbull states in the refrain that the "deep," "wild," and "silent" Mayflower gulch was inhabited by wolverines and wildcats, but men were perhaps the most dangerous creatures there. The indictment of these men stands in direct contrast to the fondness with which she writes about other fictional mountain folk: Mr. Probus, Ike and Delia Jesser, Dee Ann Jesser, Ike Buffin, Leafy Buffin, John Dorn, Min Shantallys, her son Mark, and others. Her collected works may be slim, yet her fictional Insiders still convey quite a rich world.

Turnbull's protagonists all reflect her deep love of the mountains, a love in which the landscape assumes its own force in their lives. In fact, it is their implicit love of both the grandeur and the minutiae of the high country that determines the course of their lives. As we began, let's return to *Goldboat* and *The Far Side of the Hill*, quite different stories that are nonetheless similar in their beginnings and endings. *Goldboat* is the tale of John Dorn, who comes from the East to build and manage a mining dredge funded by an avaricious company run by President Samuel Ditmar, who is also the father of Alicia, Dorn's love interest. Dorn strikes up a friendship with the reputable local, Ike Buffin, who runs the sawmill and has a daughter, Leafy. It is largely a tale of gold mining, but in the process of building the "boat" Dorn begins to see Alicia more clearly. When she comes from the East to visit, he urges her to take a look at the operation. She is averse to both the conditions of mountain life and to the conditions of the operation. During her visit to the gold dredge it is her squeal which sets off a chain of events that results in a man losing his life. Dorn realizes the greed that drives Ditmar's decisions about the operation, and he begins to understand his growing love for the mountain and the mine. Dorn possesses the integrity that Ditmar lacks. At novel's end, Dorn's relationship with Alicia is finished and he realizes that he now loves Leafy, a mountain girl born and raised. Throughout the novel, Leafy is associated with the scent of balsam, the sturdy pine, green year round.

The Far Side of the Hill spins a similar, tale. Ike and Delia Jesser have a small home in Topas, but in the summer months they move closer to timber line to be near the mine which Ike works. Dee Ann, who has just graduated from school and has no plans yet, is their only daughter. Dee Ann meets a wealthy stranger who is camping near the tree line, and within a week, after an argument with her mother, she runs away with him. He takes her to Denver and Colorado Springs where they stay in plush lodgings, and he overwhelms her with clothes and other material possessions. Dee Ann grows increasingly miserable, and when her father sends her a ruby that he dug by hand from the mine she realizes where she belongs. She returns to Topas, and the novel hints that she will marry Mark Shantallys, a boy Dee Ann's age who is also born and raised in Topas. Again, a love of the mountain range is an unspoken, necessary ingredient for a successful relationship between the young man and woman. In both novels young people realize they belong with a partner who loves not only life in the mountains, but the mountains themselves. While Turnbull is never overtly didactic about it, their mutual love for the novel's setting magnetically draws them together.

Turnbull's love of the terrain, the people, the flowers, the trees, and the very air of Summit County fuels her verse. It was a sacrifice and a hardship to live year-round in the mountains, but this was her choice, a choice she made for a geography she loved. She did not aspire to write merely about this landscape, but to create a language made from it as much as she could, even if she knows that is impossible. In this she is a poet of the American sublime:

> Intolerable the marching of this range,
> This fugue of sight unbroken and immense,
> In theme and counterpoint forever strange,
> Forever overflowing human sense.
> ("Window on the Range," TMR 35; UM 85)

The range in its immensity marches beyond the lover's comprehension.

In "Dialog," Turnbull tenderly writes of one small certainty she can grasp, a fleeting "amber" moment in a small house in her beloved high country. And in this dialog with herself, she crafts a cunning sonnet that mixes her domestic love with her sublime vision, leaving her mark on her mountain home at the same time as she lets it remake her and her very words:

> Let's step outside in the mountain night, renew
> Whole vision of this integer of cells:
> This house, in separate amber shining so,
> Uniquely seen, as though another self:
> Unit in space, now for a time clearly
> Walled, roofed, warmed: now for a time...
> *How little, how long? Whisper it flawless, dare we?*
> Shout it, and count the neighbor rays that shine,
> Digits of oneness, careless into space...
> *Yet if tomorrow, yet if tomorrow shaken,*
> *Lightless, forlorn?*
>   Therefore. Look, while the eyes
> Know this for ours, and the amber word still spoken.
> Though wood shall rot and light shatter, though
> Self dissolve on a breath, this house is now.
>
>   (TMR 36; UM 86)

Whisper it flawless, dare we?

WORKS CITED

Jones, Landon Y. "On the Trail of Nabokov through the American West." *The New York Times*, 24 May 2016, www.nytimes.com/2016/05/29/travel/vladimir-nabokov-lolita.html

McCracken Robert, and Karen Fisher, editors. *Belle Turnbull, Voice of the Mountains: an Anthology.* Marion Street Publishing Co, 2004.

BELLE TURNBULL: POET UNDER QUANDARY

Uche Ogbuji

UCHE OGBUJI, born in Calabar, Nigeria, lived in Egypt, England, and elsewhere before settling near Boulder, Colorado. A computer engineer and entrepeneur by trade, his poetry chapbook, Ndewo, Colorado *(Aldrich Press, 2013) is a Colorado Book Award Winner and a Westword 2015 Award Winner ("Best Environment Poetry"). Ogbuji hosts the* Poetry Voice *podcast.*

The charm of Belle Turnbull's adopted home of Breckenridge, Colorado grows out of ore chipped from a lode under paradise. It wasn't long after an unlikely love for snowboarding overtook me, and before I knew about Turnbull, that a sampling of Colorado resort towns brought me to this place. I walked the streets along the Blue River, which rises by Quandary Peak, high mogul of the Ten Mile Range and one of Colorado's famous fourteeners, peaks more than fourteen thousand feet above sea level. Around 1860, placer gold was discovered in this area and gold bars were the piper tune that brought American colonists to Colorado. The state's history for the past 150 years is written in the impossible and infuriating stories of prospectors, adventurers and robber barons.

In her 1940 verse novel, *Goldboat,* Turnbull wrote of the moment a later arrival to this gold country caught a glimpse of the promise that had brought him:

That day when the boat came alive with the steam in her
   gauges
And the bucketline moved and bit, and roily water
Seethed round the ladderlines, and the first bucket
Rode up out of the well cramful and splashing,
John Dorn wore plastered on the sweat of his forehead
One of those discs in triumph.

(GB 23)

In describing the first find of goldflake from an eagerly pursued
prospect, the initial couple of lines overflow before settling back
into the blank verse which is the novel's standard. These lines
convey the pecuniary awe and enthusiasm that have brought
Dorn to town, however prosaic the subject may be in itself. At
the same time, the Rocky Mountain setting is never far away
from any human activity:

The old Savoy maintains a dimmed façade,
And over the raddled dotage of its cornice
Five high horns of the Great Divide stand blowing.

(GB 4)

My earliest memories of poetry come from another place
of genius. In 1985, at a too-young age, I was parceled
off to the University of Nigeria at Nsukka, the iconic town of
West African intellectuals among the anthills of the savannah,
as Chinua Achebe immortalized them. I was supposed to be
studying electronic engineering, but somehow I found myself
among a group of other engineering, maths, and science students
who became obsessed with poetry.

Our particular little group was just one of many schools and
factions of artists, poets, and performers at Nsukka, and perhaps
because we were not of the curriculum, we tended to take things
on our own terms, looking with fresh eyes at whatever preoccupied
the literate in that time and place. We hadn't much time for the
standard post-colonial views and narratives and took to forge our

[173]

own, testing our mettle where so many rubbed forearms, at the legendary Anthill Club of Nsukka. The ghostly and living voices there were explosive and there were exuberant disagreements across artistic factions.

Several years later, having abruptly left this setting in 1990, during the flight of Nigeria's middle class from the mess left by successive military dictatorships, I wandered for much of my time in the US craving such a poetic community, the feuds and friendships, exultances and embarrassments. I found lukewarm equivalents in the online world, but nothing to approach the energy of the Anthill days. Then snowboarding brought me to Colorado, and the glory of its landscape held me here beyond my initial impulse, not unlike Turnbull's John Dorn:

> He was filled and drunken
> With the thin bright wine of hours in the high country.
> Glacier-scratch and fissure, moraine and channel
> Swung in his brain together. He stood awhile
> Under the snowgleam, under peak and saddle
> Till the breath choked in his throat. This air, this country
> Would lift you up on the wings of a strong bird flying.
>
> (GB 5)

I discovered the communal echo of the Anthill days among Colorado poets who shared the same experience of being filled to bursting under mountains, and who strove for poetry that could convey a soupçon of such experience. One of these poets, David J. Rothman, introduced me to Turnbull's relatively unknown, tumbling, knotty verse, written in well-tutored metrics, but full of a character that is always breaking out of the form.

There are schools of poets in places like Boulder, Denver, and Colorado Springs which seem to have far more in common with the schools of the coasts, but my affinity is with other groups, less geographically concentrated, but coalescing on occasion to great effect, whose overriding characteristic is awe of the land, its ecosystems, its endurance on scales stretching back to pre-colonial times, even in geologic terms. If the twentieth century saw the psychologist take a firm hold on American poetry, I have found myself at home among poets who seem intent on wresting back the reins of the art for the shaman. And Turnbull captures this spirit as powerfully as any poet of this region I have yet encountered, both in *Goldboat* and in her lyrics, such as "Foreword," the first poem in *The Tenmile Range*:

> Needs must harry the Tenmile now:
> Hot in the channels behind the bone
> The words are up and the drum beats over,
> The drum beats over, the words must go.
>
> Never along that range is ease:
> Things are warped that are too near heaven,
> Ink runs clotted down the pen,
> Verse has the twist of timberline trees.
>
> (TMR 11; UM 70)[1]

But even such an inspired tribe has the human tendency of reaching for its elders. The Anthill poets devoured and debated Christopher Okigbo, Wole Soyinka, Chinua Achebe, Peters, Brutus, Okara, Awoonor, Senghor, Cesaire, and more. Like anyone else as fevered both by American terrain and by poetry, I had wondered about the Colorado poets who came before. Of course there is Kathy Lee Bates's "America The Beautiful," a poem written at Pike's Peak, and set to music so beautifully that it's a scandal this song has not become the national anthem. After some time I learned of Colorado Poet Laureate Alice Polk Hill and saw the words of Thomas Hornsby Ferril etched at a monument to Denver's origins at Confluence Park and in the State Capitol rotunda. There were glimpses of sparkle there, but nothing that could inspire the degree of interest around Okigbo, Soyinka and such from my early days.

---

[1] Lines from this poem appear as the epigraph to *The Last Midwife*, a 2015 novel by Sandra Dallas. In her acknowledgments she expands on how reading Turnbull's *The Tenmile Range* inspired her novel of an 1880s midwife in a small Colorado mining town.

Though I came late to reading her, Turnbull was hardly unheralded in the mid-20th century. She won *Poetry Magazine*'s Harriet Monroe Memorial Prize in 1938 for a group of sonnets, "At That Point Mr. Probus," and was frequently published in that journal, as well as mainstream newspapers and journals (her poem, "Journey into the North" appeared in the *New York Times* in 1937). It's difficult to conceive how someone of her talent would have lapsed into such obscurity, having once achieved notice. She made such an impression on me when Rothman showed me her prize-winning Probus poems and the beginning of *Goldboat*, that I soon afterward sought out her papers at the Denver Public Library. As I went through them, it struck me how clearly the Colorado mountains served as an anchor to bold expression and expansive style which still resonates so clearly:

> The Great Divide is a full-sprung bow
> About that country, and its arrow
> Is the length of the Tenmile, notch to tip.
> Stark is the streamhead where the narrow
> Careless snowrills stop and go,
> Atlantic, Pacific, freeze or flow.
>   ("Topography," TMR 12; UM 71)

Turnbull was aware that Colorado's territory should lead to a unique phenomenology in poetry.

More than this, she was aware that she was aware. Among Turnbull's papers, in a scrapbook (BTP ff. 33), is a note where she speaks of T. H. Ferril:

> Reply to Ferril's frequent statement that mountains are after all only dirt, stone and such tangibles:

> Yes, but they are also symbols, unavoidably: his, mine, that lady-poet's who ices them over into wedding-cakes, that minister's who finds his God in one of them.

And you, Tom, confess yourself when you say it is a matter
for wonder that Helen Rich, that I, succeed in avoiding the
use of them romantically. What you really mean is inherent
in the term fancy as opposed to the term imagination;
triteness vs originality.

Helen Rich was the companion, journalist and novelist with
whom Turnbull settled in Breckenridge later in life. Coleridge's
fancy / imagination dichotomy is one about which they clearly
thought a great deal. Elsewhere, in remarks prepared apparently
as a draft for an interview, Turnbull types:

> The main difference between verse and poetry is probably
> the difference between fancy and imagination.

Turnbull's emphasis on imagination over fancy is also a key
to her ambition, which could even lead to the envy of a friend.
Earlier in on that page of notes she had typed:

> Surely there can be no doubt that Ferril is the one Colorado
> poet, maybe the one Western poet, who has developed a
> style which is wholly himself, and thus a natural to any
> theme he chooses. And the same should be said of his
> unforced and unsentimental imagery, which is functional
> and yet unearthly beautiful. These things put him above and
> apart. I envy that man bitterly.

Here we find her self-conscious, and with some anxiousness that
she is doing justice to the sort of poetry that she believes should
emerge from her beloved mountains. Even though Ferril has
praised her qualities, and she herself has mapped his praise to
the fancy/imagination distinction, she seems unsure that she is
succeeding.

During all this time, Turnbull was also certainly charting
the literary voices of the West and trying to find her place there.
Among her papers is a copy of "New Mexican Mountain,"

the Robinson Jeffers poem, probably typed out by herself. She also typed over the poem the sur-title "Indians," suggesting she was not just reading poems she admired but also thinking categorically about them. Jeffers, closely associated with the Big Sur, is one of the great voices of the West. We can imagine Turnbull impatiently pacing the mindscapes of poets stretching from Ferril and Jeffers to D. H. Lawrence, who spent time in the Sangre de Christo mountains of New Mexico near the Colorado border, to her contemporary Myron Broomell of Durango, whom she also praised in her papers, and many more, as she refined that imagination she sought to apply to her own mountains. Like all great poets, Turnbull was always gauging her own work among her forbears and contemporaries.

Turnbull is admirably adroit with meter and rhyme. Perhaps because my coterie of Nsukka poets were outliers who were not there for a liberal arts education, we found ourselves staunchly against the prevailing modernist obsession with destroying the traditional poetic forms. Many post-colonial intellectuals saw breaking the pentameter (in Pound's terms), and everything else near it, as an important part of recovering our own heritage. This always seemed silly to us in the first place. You can hardly reclaim African heritage by continuing to write in the colonist's tongue, and free verse in English is as European as meter.

We too dreamt of emulating the effort of Ngugi wa Thiong'o to write in our own tongues (a fanciful idea in my own case until I improved my command over Igbo, Efik, or Umon). His great book of essays *Decolonising the Mind* had just arrived and it spread gunpowder over every conversation among our group, and across other groups of literati. But partly as a result of this movement, things changed in surprising ways. Kenya's education ministry had around that time suppressed the teaching of Shakespeare in schools. This was a scandal to me, and also to Kenya's president Daniel Arap Moi, who agitated to have him restored, and to many of Africa's independence leaders who had studied at

Makerere University in Uganda, where Shakespeare was heavily emphasized. Alumnus and later president of Tanzania Julius Nyerere "was translating *Julius Caesar* and *The Merchant of Venice* into Swahili in spare evening moments during the very years that he was taking his country from British colony to independent nation and then to grand experiment in African socialism" (Wilson-Lee 163).

Ultimately we reasoned that as long as we were writing in English it was quixotic to tilt against devices which had brought unprecedented success to the language. This experience cemented in me a lifelong devotion to rhyme and meter, to finding paths to post-colonial revolution within these, rather than entirely outside their magic. Much of the Colorado pioneer poetry of, say, Alice Polk Hill, was in rhyme and meter, but often of the most worn and pedestrian make. Ferril, as Turnbull observed, brought the first glimmerings of poetry rippling with the granite muscles of the Rockies. Turnbull took things even further, bringing an almost Joycean skill in idiosyncratic manipulation of syntax and diction for effect. This is something to which I myself have aspired since long before I'd heard of her, so reading the riot of expression in her poetry brought the additional delight in finding an antecedent in a characteristic poetry of Colorado which innovates within the rhyme and meter framework:

> "Duck under," she cried, "here comes
> My maidenhood down the grade again on the rampage!
> (GB 25)

Goldboat is the vehicle in which Turnbull hopes to express the many characteristic voices of ordinary people of the mountains. In the lyrical opening passage she describes the arrival of Dorn in the town of Rockinghorse, a cypher for Breckenridge, and as Leafy Buffin, another key character, observes him, she also observes the Black American cook he has brought along. She speaks to her father:

> "Don't you worry," she told him, "never you worry.
> Here's your biscuits, here's your beef ajuicing,
> I bet his darkey never cooked anything sweeter."
>
> (GB 4)

On the same page the narrator breezily speaks of how Dorn "Herded his nigger like a broody hen / To nest in the cubbyhole the boys had fixed her." This is Thedus, the great chorus and oracle of the book. After the passage quoted above, when Dorn has affixed the first disc of gold yielded from his gold dredge to his forehead with the profuse sweat of that day's work, he marches back home and is greeted by Thedus in consciously rendered demotic:

> "The golden calf,"
> She wailed upon him. "Oh you goan to turn
> Under these eyes to a bellerin golden calf.
> Oh and I folluh you thu the wildeness,
> Oh and suffah the gallopin wind upon me
> To behole the mark of the beass."
> "Oh hush up, Thedus,"
> He told her gaily. "You were sired by a hardshell Baptist
> Out of a jungle cat. If this leaf's a sign,
> It's a sign my boat is digging.
>
> (GB 23-24)

Here is a delicate matter, especially in our 21st century with its admirable but sometimes exaggerated sensitivity about language regarding minorities and oppressed people. Turnbull rarely mentions Native Americans, but when she does, it's also in terms of brusque stereotype. I am not best positioned to assess the effect of such passages on appreciation of the book. Despite having lived in the US for a couple of decades now, and having done my primary school in Europe and the US, I spent my most formative years in Nigeria, where racial tensions seemed a distant curiosity compared to our far more immediate ethnic divisions. I find it easy to place at a distance such matters as the harsh language and caricatured treatment of Thedus.

I think even among people entirely brought up in the US, however, it's accepted that if the author portrays characters with overall humanity, specific infelicities can be pardoned. The signal example in American letters is that of Nigger Jim from Mark Twain's *Adventures of Huckleberry Finn*. Thedus is not quite as prominent in *Goldboat*, but she is a powerful sage in the book, and in passages throughout has some of the catalytic effect of the Greek chorus. Turnbull puts nuggets of street sense from a hardrock country perspective into the mouth of another character, Ike Buffin, but it's into Thedus's mouth that she puts the most deeply wise and prophetic statements of the book, and she would not place so much of the dramatic weight of her story on a personality she despises. Her racially-tinged language would hardly have raised an eyebrow in 1940 when *Goldboat* was published, and it will not do to indict Turnbull upon 21st century mores for the error of being a woman of her early 20th century times. These blemishes also come in fleeting patches, and do not dominate the book.

Rothman was careful to warn me, and others, of these potential sores as he was introducing Turnbull. If in so many ways, she seemed so well qualified to be one of the great, spiritual presences in our present-day community of poets, I was briefly compelled to consider the question of whether this was an elder who would have accepted me, and acknowledged my place within her legacy, and also the question of whether this was relevant. I'm satisfied that there is no obstacle, and in fact I'm grateful for the substance of Thedus, summing up in so many ways the essential conflict of the book, between attachment to industry, which brings so many to the Rocky Mountains, and the utter unbuckling of such schemes and pretensions, insisted upon by this demanding terrain:

> "Ain't but one thing here. I see a gole gate
> An I see a hawny gate."

(GB 74)

Here, at the climax of the story, Thedus shades the Homeric parable of the gates of ivory (gold in her apt metonym) and horn, from which false and true dreams issue. The poet immediately carries the joke well over ten yards, beyond the Odyssean first down, by writing about "passing through the horny gate," as the priapic connotations of the word "horny" were well attested by the end of the 19ᵗʰ century.

Turnbull makes gold leaf into a telling symbol, referenced throughout the book for the careful reader. For Turnbull, this is not an obsession endemic to Goldboat:

> There was meat and miniver,
> Buckskin and beaver fur.
> When these had strained away
> Goldflake sifted from the poke.
> Twice raped and rough with scars
> Freehold, gone lean and grey,
> Stands at the end of wars.
>
> ("History," TMR 15; UM 74)

Mentions of gold leaf or goldflake are scattered throughout Turnbull's work; this is natural considering her association with the Blue River, and her time spent in the Breckenridge Town Hall researching for *Goldboat* the area's lively history of placers, lode mines, gold dredges, and the picayune characters surrounding these.

Colorado has seen extraordinary immigration in recent years, a time when different sorts of economy from mineral and energy extraction have taken hold. Dot com millionaires arrive in the mountain towns in refuge from Silicon Valley. Middle-class professional families from flatland suburbs combine idyllic vacations at the resorts with house hunting trips, and if they move, they import the considerable purchasing power of the service economy (I'm one of them). Scientists and accomplished artists from the world over arrive in Boulder and other university towns. The libertarian ("Magistrate and forester / Exist forlorn in these rude airs / Where dwell the ancient liberties" ["Government," TMR 14; UM 73]), deep red Colorado ethic has started to marble with expanding cells of blue. The narrow tracks over the continental divide have given way to ever-widening interstates and state routes. Elk, mountain lion and bear find increasing difficulty in tip-toeing the spaces between national forests without slipping into the emphatic footprints of expanded settlement. Turnbull has a remarkable, pastoral sense for the scope of such changes, even though she wrote of an earlier time.

> Now from that point at center
> Shot out the giant radii of labor.
> Sixty-two feet long the stout spud timbers
> Grown from the core of ages out in Oregon
> Hillside to skidway, skidway down to sawmill,
> Sawmill to widegauge, widegauge down to narrow,
> Came edging round the hairpins over Arctic,
> Came bumping down behind the swink of oxen
> To hold the dredge at anchor.
>
> (GB 20; UM 49)

She is also sensitive to the environmental consequences:

> Daylong the driller quartered the Goose Pasture.
> The first hole rooted up the honey-flowers.
> Beside the fourth a columbine lay shattered.
> The seventh engulfed a mariposa chalice
> And in the tenth a blue fringed gentian perished.
>
> (GB 16)

Many of us who have arrived here still reach to plaster the gold leaf on our foreheads (this is not an inexpensive place to live), and get distracted with our eyes on the mountains. We all must adjudge, as Thedus formulates it, between gold and horn in order to properly find our lives in high country.

The winds that greet the new Coloradoan with a furious intimacy each spring are another signal element in *Goldboat*, and they rattle us from our cozy little boxes to pay close attention in this place that scours us with its harshness as readily as it scorches our eyes with its beauty. As Turnbull writes in "Roof":

> Days when the winds that harry the divide
> Whirl down with snow upon their devil dances,
> When atoms split in cosmic suicide,
> The roof repellent to such necromancies
> Resting upon its walls aloof, alone
> Sunders from space this safety for your own.
>
> (TMR 23)

Poetry has a crucial role to play in our culture as we make these discoveries, and in Belle Turnbull we have a poet who has expressed such matters so powerfully that those of us who come afterwards in Colorado—in America—in English—would do well to pay her the same deep attention she herself paid to her mountains and their elements and their plants and animals, and to the people who lived among them and among whom she lived.

WORKS CITED

Wilson-Lee, Edward. *Shakespeare in Swahililand: In Search of a Global Poet.* Farrar, Straus and Giroux, 2016.

BELLE TURNBULL'S WESTERN NARRATIVE

David Mason

DAVID MASON *is a professor of English at The Colorado College. His many books include* The Country I Remember *(Story Line 1996),* Ludlow: A Verse Novel *(Red Hen 2007; 2010),* Sea Salt: Poems of a Decade *(Red Hen 2014), and* Davey McGravy: Tales to Be Read Aloud to Children and Adult Children *(Paul Dry 2014). His work has appeared in* The New Yorker, The Nation, Harper's, TLS, Poetry, The Hudson Review, The Sewanee Review, The Yale Review, *and other magazines around the world. He served as Poet Laureate of Colorado from 2010 to 2014.*

----- • -----

"How far we have come to feel the shade of this tree?"
—*Thomas Hornsby Ferril*

Belle Turnbull's 1940 "novel in verse," *Goldboat*, is like so many significant poems, an eccentricity. First, it's the work of a poet few of our contemporaries will have read, a woman whose writing received some attention in her lifetime (1881-1970), but has since gone out of print and suffered neglect. She was regional, and her region—Colorado—was rarely perceived as the stuff of important literature, even in the cases of Willa Cather, Wallace Stegner and others. Turnbull published relatively little—three collections of verse and one prose novel—so she didn't arouse attention through sheer industrious bulk, as some American poets are wont to do. Furthermore, while Turnbull's accomplishment is genuine, some aspects of her work have dated, and this seems especially true of *Goldboat*, with its clumsy representations of racial and sexual relations. But despite such reservations, the book deserves attention for several reasons. First, it is an example of populist modernism, a literary strain including the likes of Carl Sandburg, Robinson Jeffers, and prose writers like John Dos Passos. Turnbull's verse novel uses not only skillful and charged blank verse, but also more fragmentary forms: notations, telegrams, business reports and the like. While it tells a very traditional tale—the plot is more like a short story from *The Saturday Evening Post* than an experimental novel—its modernist techniques complicate and enrich the verse. Turnbull's narrative can also be seen in the context of other long poems from the American West, including works by Thomas McGrath, Edward Dorn, W. S. Merwin, Gary Snyder and others—verse that incorporates a new mythos and a new geography, as well as an extension of poetry's most ancient storytelling functions.

The narrative poem, especially the "longer narrative," is a sometimes popular curiosity. On the one hand, we have the epic tradition from *Gilgamesh* to *Paradise Lost*, while on the other we have fully religious narratives like the Mahabharata and the Bible. These works use verse to tell stories or pause to give us moments of lyric illumination. Until modern times, few readers ever questioned the viability of verse as a storytelling medium. Tennyson and Longfellow excelled at both lyrics and narratives without ever feeling they were betraying some essential aspect of their art. Yet even in their time, the advent of the novel and more easily available books put poets on notice: their ancient role as storytellers would not last forever. Poe had gone so far as to declare long poems entirely contradictory:

I need scarcely observe that a poem deserves its title only inasmuch as it excites, by elevating the soul. The value of the poem is the ratio of this elevating excitement. But all excitements are, through a psychal necessity, transient. That degree of excitement which would entitle a poem to be so called at all, cannot be sustained through a composition of any great length. At the lapse of half an hour, at the very utmost, it flags—fails—a revulsion ensues—and then the poem is, in effect, and in fact, no longer such. (1)

By the twentieth century, modernism seemed to have blown narrative poetry out of the water. In our own time, quite a few poets and critics, including arbiters of taste like Helen Vendler, have declared their dislike of narrative. And one can see the point. Contemporary American verse too often comprises affectless personal narratives that make the art feel unexciting or irrelevant to readers. Furthermore, when poets completely misunderstand the nearly universal practice called "free verse," writing banal expositional prose stacked up in listless lines and expecting readers to come running—well, readers have good reason not to.

Yet modernism did not really kill fictional narratives in verse. Robinson and Frost wrote them. Jeffers wrote them. Anthony Hecht and Louis Simpson wrote them, and in my own generation the list of writers of verse narratives is very long. Novels in verse are now quite common, no more endangered than novels in prose. The question is, what makes a good novel in verse? How are stories most imaginatively rendered? When is verse most skillfully and compellingly used, and when is the poet merely typing in lines without knowing what he or she really ought to be doing?

Belle Turnbull knew exactly what she was doing. She had the skill and the delight in possibilities to make *Goldboat* an example worth study. While I don't think it is a great poem or a great example of the verse novel, I also cannot dismiss it. *Goldboat* is a milestone in the literature of Colorado, and an experiment that writers can learn from. I'm glad I read it only after I had published my own verse novel, *Ludlow*, because if I had known Turnbull's book I might have been tempted to borrow some of its techniques. As it is, our two eccentric efforts can co-exist without disturbing each other in the least.

I've written elsewhere that stories are forms, no less than sonnets and villanelles are forms. The paraphrasable part of Turnbull's story is promising. A young mining engineer, John Dorn,[1] arrives in the town of Rockinghorse (perhaps a thinly disguised Breckenridge, Colorado), to build a goldboat for a dredging operation. Goldboats were usually floated on man-made ponds as they dug into the adjacent hillsides, moving loam and peat and shale till they got down to the gold ore at bedrock. Disused dredging ponds are still visible in Colorado mountain towns like Leadville. Dorn's work in the bedrock economy of Colorado— mining—positions him between heroic and antiheroic roles. His boss, and the father of his betrothed, Alicia, is a demanding investor on the verge of bankruptcy, and Dorn encounters in the town a more freedom-loving if impoverished people. Clearly he will have to make a choice between rapaciousness and love. The choice he makes is no surprise, and perhaps that is one weakness in Turnbull's book. Her characters lack shadings and complexities.

Still, from the first pages her writing is often vigorous:

> Over the Great Divide unrolls the highway
> And cars go wagging their tails among the thunders,
> Range to range stitching, weather to weather.
> In half a day you can hem the watershed
> And rush on the prairie or race on the desert again
> Unaware of the infinite clues of legend,
> The featherstitching of roads that thread the meadows,
> Follow the gulches, follow the mountain pattern.
>
> (GB 1; UM 42)

---

[1] The name is a funny coincidence, since one of Colorado's narrative poets, the author of *Gunslinger* (1968), was Edward Dorn.

One might object to the sewing metaphor for landscape—
certainly not as fresh as Elizabeth Bishop's comparison of a fish's
skin to wallpaper—but from the opening stanza Turnbull's blank
verse rhythms are strong and active:

> There wasn't any widgeon or any rocksnake
> When young John Dorn came seething into the district
> Easing the tires of his palpitant new roadster
> Along the corduroy through the Goose Pasture,
> With his negro cook adrift and undone in the tonneau
> And a goldscale riding hard on her jellied bosom.
>
> (GB 2; UM 42)

The "negro cook," whose name is Thedus, proves both a
Hollywood stereotype, a sort of Butterfly McQueen complete
with dialect shuffling, and one of the book's more important
characters, equipped with a fortuneteller's mystical intuition.
Compare her to the adherents of obeah in Jean Rhys's novel,
Wide Sargasso Sea, and you'll see she's a thinly imagined character:

> "UH-uh," she moaned, "wasn' yo maw made me
> Swear on huh dyin bed to follow yo courses
> I suah would bandon you now. An her that's comin,"
> Her eyes went baleful, "I done run the cahds on huh,
> Queen of spades an a curse, an Thedus slavin
> Under huh lil high heels"
>
> (GB 24)

Luckily this stage vernacular does not go on for long. "Her that's
comin" is Alicia, Dorn's beloved—another character so lightly
sketched as to be barely visible. The third woman in the story is
wonderfully named, Leafy Buffin, the freedom-loving mountain
girl we get to know mainly by her attractively willful absence.
Thedus is more interesting than either of the white girls:

> Thedus wasn't paddling the lodge that evening.
> She sat pressed into a corner of her bedplace

In a strongly resinous welter of woodwaste and sawdust
And told the beads of a negro's infinite loneliness
And bonedeep surety of outrageous future.
Lost in a bleak unmellowed white man's country
She stared down the candleray.

(GB 7)

Thedus also has her cards, her fortune-telling and magic, which come in handy at the book's climactic moment of decision. Like a seer out of Greek or Roman epic, she tells Dorn that he has a choice: "I see a gole gate / An I see a hawny gate." Not ivory, but gates of gold and horn—to reach his true love, Dorn must pass through the latter.

Turnbull's love story and her protagonist's choice between two women mirrors the economic plot, which is more precisely and satisfyingly dramatized. Not only is her businessman villain more vitally alive than most other characters, but Dorn's struggle, his actual work and the hardships it entails, offers the best writing in the book. Turnbull excels as a poet of work and action. Her first departure from blank verse is in Dorn's report to his boss:

… Old volcanic mountains,
Eruptive sheets of porphyry
… Communition of values
… Drift of the ice age,
Fifty glaciers grinding
… Breaking down of fissures
Where the gold was molten
… Rich float on the benches,
Washed along the waters
… Light auriferous gravel,
Loam of the gulches
… Fine gold on the low bars,
Coarse gold in the nuggets
… Thirty million dollars
Scraped from the surface
When the place was booming

(GB 10)

In the literature of the American West the desert landscape can seem more alive than the people. Turnbull takes full advantage of alternative formats for versification, from angry telegraph dialogues between Dorn and his boss to a driller's notes and an insidious "Report to Stockholders." Imagine a minimalist version of Paul Thomas Anderson's film *There Will Be Blood*, in which ruthless commerce battles with fraudulent religion. *Goldboat* does not have so broad a canvas or so dark a vision of America, which is one reason why it feels too restrained and minor a work. Still, Turnbull understands the world of kited stocks as well as the work of geologists, diggers and watchmen. Her poem reminds us of the soulless greed that has erased so much of value in American culture and left its detritus everywhere in our land.

In my favorite parts of *Goldboat*, language itself breaks down and punctuation vanishes. This happens when Dorn feels his first romantic confusion, and again when he's in the midst of important action, trying to save everything he has built:

> The guiderope   there, under our hand   now
> Feel for the plank   Jesus what an angle
> Down into the dark   claw down   down
> Maybe next step your foot'll be in water
> What's that noise ahead   like wood chattering
> Onto wood   why that migdsht be the plank
> Hitting against the housing   busted loose
> Some chance then
>
> (GB 65; UM 62)

The writing responds to pressure and urgency, as it often should in prose fiction. But a longer narrative poem is not just a string of well-written moments. It has to fill the psychological space of its characters and its dramas, and its lyricism needs to rise above the story on occasion, lifting us to some place we could not find by other means. Readers may disagree about whether Turnbull's restraint is too limiting, whether her story needed just a bit more spark and wildness.

———•———

Turnbull was born in New York State, and moved with her
family to Colorado Springs at the age of nine. She worked
as a school teacher, retiring first to Frisco, then to Breckenridge,
both mountain towns, in the late 1930s. Clearly she loved the
mountains and knew them well. We can also see this in her
1957 collection of lyrics, *The Tenmile Range*, with its sonnets and
ballad-like narratives. She would have made a fine poet laureate
for the state, I think, and was a much better writer than our first
four laureates: Alice Polk Hill (who served from 1919 to 1921),
Nellie Burgit Miller (1923-52), Margaret Clyde Robertson
(1952-54) and Milford E. Shields (1954-1975). I mention these
names partly to put her in the literary context of Colorado, but
also because I want to compare her, briefly, to our fifth poet
laureate, Thomas Hornsby Ferril (who served from 1979 to his
death in 1988). Like Turnbull, Ferrill was a notable poet who
has yet to be sufficiently recognized for his accomplishments. He
was sixteen years younger than Turnbull, but their similarities
link them as important twentieth century Colorado writers. They
were both poets of a populist-modernist tradition, masters of a
Frostian blank verse as well as other forms, adept as sonneteers,
and as attuned to the Rocky Mountain landscape as Frost was to
his adopted New England.

As I read Turnbull, I find a handful of her lyrics very fine, and
her novel in verse has moments of vivid imagination and power,
but in the best poetry the full sweep and anarchy of imagination
feel barely contained, and I do think Turnbull's imagination is
sometimes too subdued. Ferril was a more freewheeling poet by
any measure, yet he never wrote a novel in verse. So the fact of
Goldboat, the example of it as a book, a polyphonic narrative of
nearly eighty pages, is in itself remarkable. Oddly enough, I wish
the poem were longer. I wish there were scenes that opened up
the chaos and grandeur of her characters' lives, allowing us to feel
more of Leafy and Alicia, more of Thedus, and perhaps more

of Dorn's desperation to succeed. What makes Ferril a more pleasing Colorado poet to my way of thinking is his anarchic imagination, from his dialogue with a dressmaker's dummy in "Magenta" to his coyote-tour of world history in "Nocturne at Noon—1605." Here, as one small example of his work, is the lyric poem, "Morning Star":

> It is tomorrow now
> In this black incredible grass.
>
> The mountains with luminous discipline
> Are coming out of the blackness
> To take their places one in front of the other.
>
> I know where you are and where the river is.
>
> You are near enough to be a far horizon.
> Your body breathing is a silver edge
> Of a long black mountain rising and falling slowly
> Against the morning and the morning star.
>
> Before we cannot speak again
> There will be time to use the morning star
> For anything, like brushing it against
> A pentstemon,
> Or nearly closing the lashes of our lids
> As children do to make the star come down.
>
> Or I can say to myself as if I were
> A wanderer being asked where he had been
> Among the hills: "There was a range of mountains
> Once I loved until I could not breathe."
>
> (Ferril 25)

In this kind of lyric, borders between inner and outer states evaporate—the subjective is the objective, and vice versa. Narrative poems, too, can open up more of the imaginal space, more of the unparaphrasable. I wish Belle Turnbull had more often exceeded her decorum or demolished it altogether.

Yet both of these writers were strong and original artists of the West—important voices for anyone who wants to understand Colorado—and both are almost completely neglected now. It is possible to live a lifetime in Colorado unaware of Ferril's fine sonnet painted in the rotunda of the state capital. It is possible to get a high school or college diploma in the state without ever reading a line of its literary past. By the same token, it is possible to drive through the mountains without knowing their names or the names of the tribes and the peoples who have left their stories here. There are beautiful poetic voices in the story of Colorado, and without them we who live in the state cannot really know where we are. These lines from a Turnbull lyric, "Words About a Place," are part of the poetic struggle to name accurately where we live:

> But the words have not come up, they have not found
>   you,
> For a town blanched at the head of a high valley,
> For what was first out of the turf returning,
> Out of the springs, out of the strong rock,
> Never the words, only the air thinned round you.
>
> (TMR 53; UM 90)

Those scars and ruins in our landscapes all have their stories, some of them in acutely fashioned lines. They ought to be heard.

WORKS CITED

Ferril, Thomas Hornsby. "Morning Star." *Westering*, Yale UP, 1934.
Poe, Edgar Allen. "The Poetic Principle." *The Home Journal*, no. 36, 31 Aug. 1850.

NOTES AND ACKNOWLEDGMENTS

NOTES ON THE POETRY

GOLDBOAT

The bracketed titles of the Goldboat *excerpts have been added editorially to assist in navigation and discussion.*

[OPENING/DORN'S ARRIVAL]

Rockinghorse country

A fictionalized version of Breckenridge, Colorado.

placers

Placer grounds are discussed in footnote 1 on UM 132 as part of the annotations on Turnbull's biography on Charles Stanley Revett. Methods of placer mining are discussed in footnote 10 on UM 135.

Squeezem Ditmar

Mine owner Samuel Ditmar may be named in reference to Raymond L. Ditmars, author of *Snakes of the World* (1933) and *A Field Book of North American Snakes* (1939). Earlier references to rocksnakes, a North American boa subspecies not native to Colorado, suggests a further herpetological connotation to his nickname "squeezem."

TELEGRAMS [I]

Flattened nugget

In dredging, gold nuggets would be flattened between the bedrock and the dredging apparatus. See Turnbull's essay on Revett (specifically the section "The Cleanups" [UM 141]) for more information.

Bait allimportant

Nuggets such as the ones Dorn and Ditmar discuss were often used as specimens to entice potential investors. Regardless, use of the word "bait" to refer to these samples appears to be particular to Ditmar, and is not standard industry usage.

[OLSEN]

cleanup

Part of the regular maintenance cycle of a placer mining operation, the cleanup involved partially dismantling the mining apparatus. In addition to clearing sediment away from the machinery, this frequently allowed the reclamation of a significant quantity of gold that may have slipped through the cracks. The period of time between cleanups varied from twenty-days to four months, depending on the scale and needs of the operation (*Placer Mining* 117-18).

A thin, triangular, red, drifted over the sump.
> Compare this to Turnbull's description of a similar event that occurred in one of Revett's operations (UM 142).

Telegrams [V]
Loved I not honor
> A reference to 17th century English poet Richard Lovelace's 1649 poem, "To Lucasta, Going to the Warres:" The last two lines read, "I could not love thee, Dear, so much, / Loved I not honour more."

The Tenmile Range

Time as a Well-Spring
Gassed and sent in again and lined with lead
> According to Whittington (and the staff of the Mining Hall of Fame, many of whom have worked in Colorado's mines), "gas" not only refers to an excess of "bad air" (carbon dioxide, carbon monoxide, etc.) but to common, mine-specific pollutants, such as the smoke from blasting powder. The reference to lead is more of a mystery. Historically, molybdenum has often been confused with lead. Else, Probus may be expressing apprehensions regarding the lead deposits that would be present in the mine in addition to molybdenum. In 1932 (five years before this poem's publication) there had been a lead-poisoning epidemic in Baltimore that had made national headlines.

to stand the gaff
> Rothman addresses the origins of this phrase in his essay (UM 24).

Lunch Time in the Tunnel
pumps
> The pumps here are likely not for ventilation, as would be assumed, but for keeping the mines from flooding. Despite the high elevation in Leadville, an equally high water table means that the flooding of mines is a real and persistent obstacle in Colorado mining (Whittington).

In those Rude Airs
Sagehen
> Likely referring to the female of the Gunnison Sage-Grouse (*Centocercus minimus*), noted for a brown throat and breast, a dark belly, and long, pointed tail feathers (Alderfer 47).

TRAILS

The poems in Turnbull's last book, Trails, *are all drawn from* The Long Arc—*a book-length collection she had assembled for publication, but never found a market for. Additional poems from this unprinted volume are reproduced here* (UM 110-119); *the entirety may be found in her papers.*

IN THE JOYFUL MODE

a rhyme may leap for wantonness

Emended yellow copy in BTP ff. 12, made in preparation for *The Long Arc*, reads "a rhyme may strut for wantonness." However, as the publication of *Trails* postdates this, the line is kept as it appears there.

UNPUBLISHED OR UNCOLLECTED POEMS

SONNET TO GERTRUDE BUCK

Originally published in Vassar Quarterly, *vol. 7, no. 4 (July, 1922).*

Gertrude Buck, Ph.D. (1871-1922), was a noted rhetorician who taught numerous courses at Vassar in a variety of subjects such as English, literary theory, poetics, rhetoric and composition, and drama. Pedagogically, she was distinguished by an approach which anticipated modern rhetoric and composition studies by prioritizing means of addressing unequal power structures, rather than focusing on grammatical rules to be memorized by rote (cf. Bordelon).

SONG FOR FEMALE VOICES

Originally published in Voices: A Journal of Verse, *vol. 3, no. 2 (Mar.-Apr., 1922).*

MOUNTAIN-MAD

Originally published in Voices: A Journal of Verse, *vol. 3, no. 2 (Mar.-Apr., 1922) with all lines aligned to the left margin. Reprinted in the* Denver Post *on April 3rd of the same year, with the slightly more varied justification we reproduce here.*

RECKONING

Originally published in The Midland: A Magazine of the Middle West, *vol. 11, no. 16 (Sep. 15, 1925).*

There yet remain the mountain and the moon

In *The Midland*, "remains" was published instead of "remain." In her archived copy of it (BTP), an unknown hand (presumably Turnbull's) has crossed out the offending "s."

[Weather Report]
The title comes from the white archived copy (BTP ff. 12), however, in the yellow copy emended in preparation for this poem's inclusion in The Long Arc, *Turnbull has crossed this title out. It is not clear if she had another title in mind, or if she wished the poem to remain untitled.*

Now the Slow Dawn
When this was published in the April 29, 1938, issue of The Commonweal, *the title was repeated in the first line. However, in BTP ff. 12, Turnbull typed it in the manner we have reproduced here—with the repeititon of the title in the first line only suggested by sufficient whitespace.*

No Other Water
whether they come from shaft or schoolhouse
> In BTP ff. 15, the yellow copy is emended from "whether they come from shaft or sawmill."

So what must she choose for mate of her Junetime?
> Emended from "So what was her choice for mate of her springtime?"

down off our basin, out and again;
> Emended from "down off our basin, out and away;"

Inward Tussle for a Couple of Lines
and
Never the Words (a monlog) [variant]
Both of these poems are variations of "Never the Words (A MONOLOG)" (T 15; UM 103).

Delinquent Tax List of Summit County
High up the Valley of the Blue,
> The copy in the BTP ff. 20 is emended from "High in the Valley of the Blue."

Gold boats munching up the Swan, / Digging the pits they floated on,
> Emended from "Gold boats munching along the Swan, / Digging the pools they floated on."

Glory holes in Farncomb Hill
> In the foreword to the unpublished anthology she was compiling (BTP ff. 17) Turnbull herself supplies this definition for *glory hole*: "To Western hardrock miners, a gloryhole is a pocket in the rock where much free gold has been found."

"Not to be published [during my lifetime]"
All of the poems in this section are found in BTP ff. 22, under the heading we have given them here. The bracketed part of the title has been heavily scored out by hand, but is still faintly legible. Rothman speaks to their context and the rationale for their inclusion on UM 26.

CHANT

blue–black monkshood

Referring to *Aconitum columbianum*, a forest plant of the *Helleboraceae* family, recognizable by the uppermost sepal forming a hood over a blue-purple flower (Weber and Wittman 215).

sky–bright mertensia

Could refer to any plant of the *Mertensia* genus, part of the *Boraginaceae* family. Commonly referred to as the chiming bell or bluebell, the flowers resemble inverted, funnel-shaped bells, ranging in color from sky- to royal-blue (Weber and Wittman 119).

WORKS CITED EDITORIALLY

Alderfer, Jonathan, editor. *Complete Birds of North America*. National Geographic Society, 2006.

Bordelon, Suzanne. *A Feminist Legacy: The Rhetoric and Pedagogy of Gertrude Buck*. Southern Illinois UP, 2007.

OED Online. Oxford UP, 2000-17, www.oed.com

Placer Mining: A Handbook for Klondike and Other Miners and Prospectors. Colliery Engineering Company, 1897.

Van Bueren, Thad M. "A 'Poor Man's Mill': A Rich Vernacular Legacy." *IA: The Journal of the Society for Industrial Archaelogy*, vol. 30, no. 2 (2004): pp. 5-23.

Weber, William A., and Ronald C. Wittman. *Colorado Flora: Eastern Slope*. 3rd ed., Colorado UP, 2001.

Whittington, Steve [Director of the Mining Hall of Fame]. "Re: The Probus Poems." E-mail received by Jeffrey R. Villines, 14 Feb. 2017.

ABOUT THE EDITORS

DAVID J. ROTHMAN serves as Director of the Graduate Program in Creative Writing at Western State Colorado University, where he also directes the Poetry Concentration, edits the journal *THINK* and directs the annual conference Writing the Rockies. His most recent volumes of poetry, both of which appeared in 2013, are *The Book of Catapults* (White Violet) and *Part of the Darkness* (Entasis). His poems and essays have appeared in journals such as *Agni*, *The Atlantic Monthly*, *The Hudson Review*, *The Kenyon Review*, *Poetry*, and scores of others. He serves on the board of the Association of Writers and Writing Programs (AWP).

JEFFREY R. VILLINES is a Ph.D. student in literature at the University of Houston. He holds an M.A. in English from the University of Virginia and a B.A. in English, Theatre, and Russian from Ouachita University. He has previously worked with Documents Compass to assist in the transcription and digitization of the papers of the Early American Presidents.

ACKNOWLEDGEMENTS

Both editors wish to thank Unsung Masters Series curators Wayne Miller and Kevin Prufer; the staff of Pleiades Press, especially Kathryn Nuernberger; the Staff of the Mining Hall of Fame in Leadville, Colorado, especially Stephen Whittington; the staff of the Western History Collection at the Denver Public Library, especially Coi Drummond-Gehrig, Jim Kroll, and Abby Hoverstock; Karen Fischer and Robert McCracken, who preceded us as editors of Turnbull's work by publishing the ebook anthology *Belle Turnbull: Voice of the Mountains* and a facsimile of *The Tenmile Range*; UH English Department Chair J. Kastely; and UH Creative Writing Director Alex Parsons. David also wishes to thank Professor Patty Limerick, the Faculty Director of the Center of the American West at the University of Colorado at Boulder, for introducing him to Janet Robertson, who insisted he read Belle Turnbull. He also wishes to thank Tony Hoagland, who presented the idea of the book to Kevin Prufer and Wayne Miller at Pleiades Press; his co-editor, Jeffrey Villines, for his extraordinary work in a challenging year; all the contributors to the book, each of whom has done so much for Colorado poetry; and his wife Emily and sons Jacob and Noah for their love and support. Jeff wishes to thank David Vander Meulen for his bibliographic preparation (and for helping with a couple textual challenges), Natalie M. Houston for diligently teaching version control, David Rothman and Kevin Prufer for bringing him onto this project (Kevin also let him monopolize his office computer to set the text of this volume), Andre Cobb for helping arrange an indispensible research trip, Martin Rock for his excellent designs, and of course, Alli—his wife of eight years and proofreader of ten.

This book is produced as a collaboration
between Pleiades Press and
Gulf Coast: A Journal of Literature and Fine Arts.

GENEROUS SUPPORT AND FUNDING PROVIDED BY:

Cynthia Woods Mitchell Center for the Arts
Houston Arts Alliance
University of Houston
Missouri Arts Council
University of Central Missouri
National Endowment for the Arts

This book is set in Adobe Caslon Pro type
with Ostrich Sans Inline and Dense titles.

Designed by Martin Rock,
Typeset by Jeffrey R. Villines